Contents

	Commendation	3
	Foreword	5
	Prologue	7
1	Crisis in the church	9
2	A tattered treasure	19
3	The shopping list	31
4	They pray about everything	39
5	We've never been taught to pray	51
6	Prayer is the heart of the church	61
7	This is the kind of preaching we need	67
8	We cannot lose in the praying business	77
9	Everything but prayer	87
10	The prayer meeting is for the glory of God	97
11	Trouble focuses the mind	107
12	The Lord chastens those whom He loves	117
13	God can bring good out of apparent disaster	123
14	Heart trembling is not always a sign of unbelief	135
15	I don't know exactly what to pray for	143
16	Ye have not, because ye ask not	153
17	Lord, I must have a word from Thee	161
18	How can a Christian oppose a man of God?	167
19	Ten lepers were healed . . . only one went back to give thanks	181
20	'Blest be the tie that binds' has become a meaningless phrase	187
21	Lord, teach us to pray	197
22	A praying pulpit begets praying pews	203
23	Call upon me in the day of trouble: I will deliver thee	211

Commendation

If the church prayer meeting is the thermometer of the congregation's life, many of our churches would have a lot of heart searching to do. It is this vital theme which has prompted Jim Handyside to write the book which is now in the reader's hands.

Convinced as the author is that reform and revival of the local congregation are related to the degree of earnestness in the prayers of God's people, Pastor Handyside has set out to do what every pastor could wish to have attempted: a book designed to promote real scriptural and heartfelt prayers in the members of a church.

Melt the Icebergs! is a pastor's imaginative portrayal of how one church—the country might be Britain, America, or elsewhere—finds its way from a state of dead formalism into a new era of blessing. The story is fictional but the scenario fits almost anywhere today. The author is committed to the doctrines of grace and makes no apology for introducing the reader to several of the best books on theology and prayer available today. The author is cessationist in his view of the *gifts,* but he is committed firmly to a belief that mighty things are wrought in prayer—sometimes even wonderful healings, when that is God's sovereign will.

The story takes us through a painful, as well as joyous

3

experience, in the life of a local church. We are reminded that "there is no trouble like church trouble." We see the carnality of the human heart as well as the sweetness of mature spirituality. And the charm of true romance is not absent in this very human and modern story.

But the main lesson is that we are all beginners in the school of prayer and that we had better all take a lowly and a teachable place if we are to make progress in that vital area of our lives as Christians. The present writer, though he is accustomed to meetings for prayer which differ somewhat from those envisaged here, puts his own name down first among those who are willing to be taught. He hopes that many others will be willing to follow him and find timely help from this interesting book.

If Pastor Handyside's labors in writing this story serve to draw attention to the general need to become more biblical and more spiritual in our prayer meetings, his endeavors will be amply rewarded. We fervently hope this is what will take place.

Rev. Maurice Roberts
Free Greyfriars Manse, Inverness
Editor, *Banner of Truth* magazine

Foreword

The church in the latter part of the twentieth century is suffering many woes, but none as serious as the weakness she displays in prayer. Whether in corporate prayer or individual prayer, both areas are falling far short of the teaching and example of our Lord and Scripture.

We are committing two very serious errors concerning prayer as reflected in James 4:2-3. First, we do not pray (*Ye have not, because ye ask not*). Second, when we do pray, we don't really know how to pray or what to ask for (*Ye ask, and receive not, because ye ask amiss*). Clearly, the church as a whole and individual Christians are badly in need of instruction concerning prayer.

That is why my heart is thrilled at the publication of the present manuscript from the pen of my dear brother, Jim Handyside. He attacks the problem of the church today in these areas of prayer. Yet he does it in a very unique manner—by means of a theological novel. Through the lives of true-to-life characters, and through the life of the church, he shows us from a crisis situation the solutions to the greatest problems of the church and of the individual in this matter of prayer. The reader will immediately identify with the people and the church life he presents in this work, which actually is more than a novel—it is a manual on prayer, full of practical instruction and encouragement to every believer who longs for his life and his church to be powerful in the arena of prayer.

Not only is the book unique in its format of a theological novel, but it is also unique as it has grown from the heart of a man who has experienced the truths he presents. This is not a book on the theory of prayer from one who has read the books of others and now synthesizes their convictions. This is a book from the heart of a man who has wrestled in the arena of prayer in his own personal life, seeking to know and be in prayer what Scripture reveals a believer should be. This is a book from the heart of a man who as a pastor has longed for and sought to make the church he pastors mighty and fervent in prayer (something unique in our day). Though he would be the first to admit that he has not arrived in fullness in these areas, anyone around him for a period of time clearly sees the dedication and heartbeat and burden he has for the subject.

Truly this book is a must for the church as we close this twentieth century and enter the next. What could be greater than for the church to enter the twenty-first century with a transformed and biblical prayer life?

Dr. Richard P. Belcher
Prolific Author, Pastor, Preacher
Professor of Theology, Bible, Greek
Columbia International University
Columbia, South Carolina

Prologue

The author is well aware that gatherings for prayer in the evangelical church assume many different forms and structures, modes of address and posture. The main aim of this book is not particularly to address these issues, but to concentrate on the Biblical principles, especially relating to corporate prayer. It is to be hoped that any differences in these realms which the reader may encounter from his own experience, will not inhibit serious consideration of the basic emphasis of the book. Although situated in the United Kingdom, I believe that the principles espoused, are capable of universal application.

It is surely a phenomenon of some import that the subject of the necessity of vital prayer is one that all shades of evangelical opinion can find much mutual agreement upon, as perhaps they cannot on many other subjects or doctrines. Yet, sadly, this fundamental need is relegated to minimal practice, consideration, or discussion. The lack of ministry relating to the subject of prayer, from church pulpit to Conference platform, is surely one of the great tragedies of the modern church. If this is coupled to a general absence of teaching to the present generation of Christians on the vital subject of how to pray, either personally or corporately, then we might have some indication of a major reason why the church has succumbed to so much humanistic philosophy and pragmatism in the contemporary apostate age, leading often to the relegation of the prayer meeting as an anachronism in modern evangelical church life.

Pastor Jim Handyside
Reformed Baptist Church
Anniesland, Glasgow
Scotland

1

Crisis in the church

"Bill, I haven't seen you so agitated about a phone call from the church in all the twenty years we've been members," Ruth exclaimed.

"No, and after ten years as a deacon in a Baptist church, you get a kind of sense when trouble is brewing," Bill remarked disconsolately. "I've tried to be conscientious in attending church meetings and in recognizing the responsibility I'm supposed to carry in setting an example for other members. Still, I feel uneasy and suspicious about this phone call."

"Well, I can't understand why you should feel uneasy or surprised to receive a phone call from the pastor. He's simply asking for an urgent meeting with James Frame and yourself. After all," Ruth continued, "Andrew Paterson is the pastor, and you and James are deacons, so I think you are being too concerned over a perfectly natural request."

"Listen, Ruth, there *is* something peculiar about this," Bill said emphatically. "I mean, why should Andrew phone during dinner and request an immediate meeting with James and me? Why the extreme urgency? I hope he hasn't heard about the rumblings of discontent among some of the mem-

9

bers regarding his ministry and the dryness of the prayer meetings!"

"Don't be silly," Ruth replied. "You haven't discussed these matters with anyone but me, and I definitely have not mentioned them to anyone else."

"You're probably right," he remarked. "But it's strange nevertheless."

Ruth responded quickly with tongue in cheek, "Maybe he thinks it's time you gave him a raise in his salary. After all, these are hard times!"

Bill treated her remark with the disdain he thought it deserved.

* * *

"Ah, good evening, men," Andrew said. "Come inside and I'll take your coats."

Bill and James Frame made their way into the neat, cozy front room with its bay window and attractive stone fireplace.

"Have a seat. Make yourselves comfortable," Andrew said affably, though Bill thought a trifle nervously. "Thanks for coming at such short notice, but I felt that the sooner we met the better."

Neither of the deacons said anything, but their curiosity was aroused even more. They looked attentively at Andrew.

"I . . . er . . . I'm not sure how to put this," Andrew stammered, as if searching for the right words. "Anyway, the fact is that I have accepted a call to another church, and of course I wanted you men to be the first to know."

James Frame coughed nervously and looked at Bill to see his reaction.

Bill found himself saying, "Well, this is a shock, Andrew. I'd no idea. What brought this on? Is there anything

10

wrong at the church, or are you dissatisfied about something?"

Ruth's jocular remark about the salary came back to Bill like an arrow, and he had to admit, she did have remarkable flashes of intuition at times!

"No, no. Definitely not!" Andrew seemed very emphatic in assuring them.

"Having prayed about it for several months, both Elaine and I feel that it's God's time for us to accept another challenge."

James Frame, who had not spoken during the exchange, asked deferentially, "Had you any specific time in mind about leaving?"

Andrew was a little edgy at this as he said, "Actually this is the hard part. Oakvale Baptist Church has been without a pastor for nearly a year, and they would like me to commence ministry there at the beginning of the month. Now I realize that this is very short notice for you, but on the other hand I have kept them waiting for several months as we prayed about it. However, if you think it's impossible for me to take up the charge so soon, then I will ask them if it could be delayed for another month."

The pastor and deacons had a brief, unconvincing word of prayer together and parted, agreeing to meet again soon to tie up the details and make arrangements for the future.

* * *

Ruth listened carefully as Bill recounted the evening's events.

"He certainly kept it dark, didn't he? Neither did Elaine ever once hint at such a thing to any of the ladies. They were always a bit secretive though, weren't they?" Ruth tailed off contemplatively.

11

"You know what's really worrying me, Ruth?" Bill said as he broke into her thoughts. "I'm not as agitated as I feel I should be at the loss of a pastor. To tell the truth, I don't even feel inclined to try and get him to postpone his departure for another month. I kind of sense that God is bringing a new start to things, and—well, just look at your text hanging on the wall there."

Ruth glanced up at the little framed embroidered text that she had sewn so many years ago: "All things work together for good to them that love God. Romans 8:28."

"It's one thing to have it hanging on the wall," Bill exclaimed, "but it's another thing altogether to exercise the faith to appropriate it when the occasion demands!" He felt quite uplifted by the little pearl of insight he had dispensed.

* * *

The next evening Bill thought as he arrived home, "I'm really glad to get home tonight." His reverie was jolted somewhat, however, when he recalled that it was Wednesday, the prayer meeting evening!

"I know I've had a hard day's work," he mused, "but I ought to have more enthusiasm for the prayer meeting tonight."

"Maybe I'm backsliding or backslidden," he thought, "because I realize that as a Christian I should be looking forward to the church prayer meeting."

Somewhat assailed by doubts and misgivings as to his spiritual condition, Bill reluctantly reminded his wife that it was time they left for church or they would be late. Bill was in a state of turmoil over the news that Andrew had broken on Tuesday evening. Earlton Baptist Church boasted about a hundred members and was fortunate in having a reasonable cross-section of the community represented in its member-ship.

"I guess we're fortunate to have had a man like Andrew in these days in spite of his faults," Bill thought, as he drove with Ruth into the church parking lot. "When you consider that he has been quite sound doctrinally and solid in his concern for evangelistic and missionary involvement."

They were first to arrive at the church, and Bill's mind was still ranging over the situation with some despondency as he entered the building. "I wonder if these events will bring James Frame out tonight?" A touch of cynicism overtook Bill as he thought, "Imagine needing a catastrophe to get you out to the prayer meeting! Anyway, would it be any encouragement if he did come?" Bill couldn't remember the last time James had prayed with other than a dull, colorless, uninspired repetition.

Just then the arrival of Andrew and several other members disturbed Bill's rather depressing line of thought. Everyone exchanged greetings and then made their way into the church to await the others.

Bill and Ruth sat near the front. To an onlooker, Bill and Ruth's silence might have been construed as preparation for the service that lay ahead. In reality, Bill's mind was drifting, again considering in somewhat unsanctified fashion the recent events.

He continued to ponder, "Why are the Smiths *always* late? Why are the same people inevitably late? Why doesn't the pastor start the meeting at 7:30 p.m. as scheduled, instead of always hanging on to accommodate these latecomers?"

A few more stragglers arrived and the pastor announced the opening hymn to the twenty or so people who were gathered.

"That's another thing," Bill thought, when he knew he

13

ought to be concentrating on the third verse of the hymn. "Why in the world do we have nearly a hundred professing members and only twenty are here this evening?"

Knowing that the deacons had agreed to hold the announcement of his departure from the congregation until further discussions, Andrew welcomed the congregation in his usual manner. He then invited them to unite in the opening prayer.

With the recent events weighing heavily on him, Bill was unsettled, his thoughts turning agitatedly over and over in his mind. "I know that I shouldn't be thinking these things, especially with Andrew going away now, but I bet he goes on and on in his normal manner for about ten minutes and I will have shut off after two! Yes! I should be concentrating, lending my support, maybe even saying 'Amen' occasionally, but why does he have to be so boring, so insensitive? I mean, doesn't the Holy Spirit ever lead him to pray briefly, or even vary his prayers in view of special circumstances?"

By this time Bill was not hearing the petitions as Andrew droned on. To be honest, he had little need to, because he could have prayed them for Andrew, so stereotyped and familiar were the words to him.

With some degree of resolution, Bill focused his mind just as Andrew gave an indication of drawing to a close at last! Opening his eyes eventually, Bill muttered to himself, "Where was it I read recently about an old Puritan who was mighty in prayer in his closet, but brief and powerful in public?" He consoled himself with the knowledge that Andrew would soon be laboring elsewhere. He tried to be balanced about it all, as he conceded to himself that doubtless there were men who could sustain intercessions for a lengthy period and yet who were apparently under the peculiar power of the Spirit.

"But, I still reckon," Bill continued ruminatively, "that they were the exception rather than the rule!"

*   *   *

Bill and Ruth left the church after exchanging pleasantries with several members, although being careful to omit any reference to Andrew's impending departure. Soon they headed home. When they were settled in their favorite armchairs with a cup of tea, Bill suddenly asked Ruth what she thought of the prayer meeting.

"What do you mean?" she asked.

"Well," Bill said uneasily, "do you think that God was in it?"

Ruth was taken aback by this blunt inquiry, but sensing that there was more behind the question than she was immediately grasping, she responded in a noncommittal way, "I didn't notice much difference about it from any other prayer meeting night."

"And that," pounced Bill, "is *exactly* what I mean. There *was* nothing different about it in spite of the upset that's about to take place in the church. The whole point of the matter is, that I'm convinced that if God were in the meeting, we would know about it, we would sense it!"

Bill began to warm to the theme expansively.

"Look," Bill went on, "I'm perfectly aware that I'm no prayer warrior, that I fall short of the biblical standards for real praying, but I am concerned to amend the situation if I can get proper help or instruction. Because of the present emergency in the church, I believe that we really need help in this area. There is a Scripture, Matthew 6:7, which has been giving me a lot of thought lately, 'But when ye pray, use not vain repetitions, as the heathen do: for they think that they shall be heard for their much speaking.'

"Now," Bill paused and, realizing that it was getting late, reassured Ruth, "let's leave it there tonight and we can discuss it again another time."

Next morning, Bill drove to the little industrial estate where he had premises housing the store and office of his modest wholesale carpet business. He had built it up from scratch and he now employed half a dozen people in various capacities.

Ron Coltart met him at the office entrance with a cheery greeting.

"Morning, Bill," Ron shouted. "Sorry I missed the prayer meeting last night, but we had a few problems at that hotel job and we didn't finish till after eight."

"Oh, too bad," Bill replied.

As he said these words, however, something else was running through his mind.

"Look at young Ron," he thought, "a comparatively new convert, young, keen, zealous. But his enthusiasm is not universally shared by the old guard. They seem to feel threatened or convicted when they compare his motivation with their own lackluster efforts."

Some time later, Bill found himself almost automatically inviting young Ron to lunch as he said, "Let's go down to the cafe and have lunch together,"

"Fine with me," Ron said airily.

Seated in the cafe at lunch time, Ron casually asked Bill about the prayer meeting and anything special that had arisen.

With approximately thirty years of Christian experience, Bill was careful not to plunge into discussion with a young convert in any way that might seem to convey veiled criticism of the church's complacent members, or the pastor's recent bombshell announcement.

16

"Well, I think it only highlighted my own sense of dissatisfaction with my prayer life and frustration with my seeming inability to progress in this particular area of spiritual growth," Bill said.

"Strange that you should mention that," Ron retorted. "I've been thinking much along these lines myself, though of course I realize that compared to you and many others in the church I'm a mere novice. Are there any Scriptures or good books that you could recommend I should study about this subject?"

Bill sighed as he said, "To be honest, Ron, I'm probably not the best person to ask because I feel that I need help in this area myself."

Bill was relieved that Ron had not asked him if he should consult Andrew on the matter. He wasn't yet free to mention Andrew's departure. Besides, how could he tell a young convert that the pastor had never demonstrated any particular gift or ability in prayer either?

18

2

A tattered treasure

"Saturday morning," Ron Coltart thought, "I'll slip into town and visit the Christian bookstore. I'm not particularly interested in the new books, but they do have a very good second hand section. Sometimes the prices are a little high, but a bargain can be obtained by perseverance and regular rummaging."

The owner of the shop was Mrs. Shearer, the widow of a pastor and missionary who had died many years before. Ron greeted her as he entered the shop. "Good morning, Mrs. Shearer, any good bargains today?"

"Ron, you know that we always have bargains here, and especially save them up for you!" Mrs. Shearer had what could only be described as very twinkling eyes. They were beady, but not unkindly so. It was just that nothing seemed to escape her attention, particularly things of a spiritual nature.

"Ron, I can hardly believe that it has been nearly a year since Bill Morgan witnessed to you at the carpet store. Time does fly, doesn't it?"

"Yes," Ron responded brightly. "The amazing thing is that the Lord has enabled me to attend almost every meeting at the Baptist church since that night."

Having kept an inconspicuous eye on young Ron since his conversion and relishing nothing more than encouraging young believers, Mrs. Shearer said, "That is a wonderful testimony, Ron."

"Thanks," he said somewhat awkwardly, not sure how to respond. "By the way, how are things going at the Bethel Mission?"

"Well," Mrs. Shearer said resignedly, "the town center is not as busy as it used to be before the new supermarket and the other shops were built on the outskirts of town at Greenfields. The work is struggling a bit now, but I do my best to be faithful as the Lord enables."

"Faithful!" Ron thought to himself. "Why she's a bulwark of that work. It wouldn't survive without her."

Ron had always found Mrs. Shearer's advice easy to receive and, upon reflection, invariably correct. He never found a *generation gap* with Mrs. Shearer in the things of God. In fact, Ron discerned, and he felt quite proud about it actually, a sign of his growing maturity. He secretly felt that Mrs. Shearer, unlike many other professing Christians that he knew, was lovingly interested in the Lord as well as His work. This was an area he felt needed correction in his own life.

Coming out of his pondering, Ron said, "Well, I don't know if I can afford anything too expensive right now, but I'll browse around."

"I think you'll be able to afford what I've laid aside for you this week, Ron," Mrs. Shearer said, with that sparkling twinkle in her eye. "Actually, I have a little present for you which was in a bundle of books I bought recently at an auction sale."

She had Ron's attention now, and he said, "Oh! what's that then?" He had been very keen to acquire several theological tomes, but could not afford them at present.

"Wow!" he exclaimed under his breath. "Maybe she's got me a Berkhof's *Systematic Theology*, or a copy of *Reformed Dogmatics* by Hoeksema. I know of that particular volume," he continued to speculate, "because I saw it recently for sale second hand at fifteen pounds, sadly out of my financial reach at the moment."

He then felt a stab of conviction at the mildly avaricious nature of his expectations and he settled himself to wait as Mrs. Shearer went into the little back room of the shop. She emerged in a moment with a slightly tattered, small paperback with a green cover and black edge. Ron fought hard to hide his disappointment, as his dream of a fine hardback doctrinal treatise evaporated. He felt decidedly uncomfortable as Mrs. Shearer, with a warm benign smile, said to him, "This, Ron, is a treasure and will amply repay careful reading and digesting."

"Oh, thanks very much," he said, trying to sound enthusiastic and grateful.

"I thought of you immediately when I set eyes on this book and also when I recalled the blessing it was to me the first time I read it," she said.

By now Ron's curiosity was definitely aroused as he took the slim volume from her hand and read the title, *The Essentials of Prayer* by E. M. Bounds.[1] He was speechless for a second.

Mrs. Shearer asked quizzically, "Is there something wrong? I know that it doesn't look like much of a treasure, but just wait till you read it."

"Er, no, it's not that," he stammered, "but Bill and I have been discussing this very subject. So this must surely be the Lord bringing some light on the matter to us."

Ron said this partly because he had once been at a prayer

meeting where Mrs. Shearer had prayed and it had left an indelible impression upon him. Her prayer seemed to flow where others appeared mechanical or wooden. He felt that if she was recommending a book on prayer so highly, it must be good.

"You read it, Ron. Then give me your thoughts," she said in her motherly way that was hard to resist. Ron thanked her and set off home with the book in his pocket and his mind in a stir.

* * *

"Wednesday evening again," Bill said a little wearily. "Time we were off to the prayer meeting." Much thought had passed through his mind since last week's meeting, and he had begun to form resolutions as a result.

"Andrew is here," Bill exclaimed to Ruth as they arrived at the church parking lot. The folks exchanged greetings as they made their way to the back hall where the prayer meeting and Bible study were generally held.

Ron came in, giving Bill a cheery nod.

"He seems pleased with himself tonight," Bill thought. "And with me having been out of town all week I haven't had a chance to talk to him for a few days."

Andrew cleared his throat and began to address the twenty odd members who were scattered throughout the hall. The front row was empty, virgin territory which had never been occupied by any of the majority who attended. The back row, on the other hand, had its collection of regulars whose names were practically engraved on their seats.

Bill's mind wandered to a fiendish plot devised in his mind, which Ruth had heard on many occasions. He often ruefully grumbled to her, "You know, Ruth, I would like to arrive really early with sufficient allies, if I could summon up such, who would occupy the back row before the regulars entered."

"Imagine . . ." he would continue with a source of smug satisfaction. "Imagine the confusion, annoyance, and disorientation such an upset would cause the poor back row residents! However, I'm convinced that there is a crafty method in this back seat occupation. There must be an unconscious sense of false security there; and anyway, who ever observed a sleeping saint on a front row seat?"

But then Andrew's familiar clearing of his throat brought Bill back to a more spiritual contemplation.

"Time for Pavlov's dogs to respond," he thought mischievously. Hurriedly remembering that he now should be in his more spiritual frame of mind, he sought to sing the first hymn with a degree of sincerity and joyfulness. He did feel a trifle exposed and lonely though, being in the second row from the front with only Ruth for company.

Bill adopted his most stoical resistance of mind to all the encroaching thoughts that flooded into his overactive brain as Andrew began the opening prayer. He was not disappointed in his prophetic forecast that this would interminably proceed in a singularly rambling fashion, practically putting to sleep the hearers. However, because it was prayer, it was sacrosanct, beyond criticism or analysis. At least to Bill's mind that seemed to be the general attitude of the church. Although the prayer was devoid of most of the necessary spiritual ingredients which the New Testament suggested were essential if it was to be heard in heaven, a critical evaluation of prayer in any shape or form was a "no-go" area![2]

"Can we turn to the second hymn," Andrew intoned monotonously.

When this was concluded, he dutifully turned to the portion of Bible study for the evening. It was a rather dry, dusty reiteration of what most fairly intelligent readers could have gleaned from the passage themselves with a little effort. Providing there is orthodoxy and no application, the message will generally receive the seal of approval from the assembled saints.[3]

How far removed this attitude all seemed from what one old saint had once confided to Bill in exasperation at a rather insipid sermon, "I never feel that I've had my money's worth out of any message unless it gets under my skin at some point!"

Bill thought, "He would certainly have felt cheated here tonight." He roused himself again and realized that these disgruntled darting thoughts hardly fulfilled the criterion of fruitful hearing.[4] He knew the lack of faith in his hearing would certainly inhibit his receiving much for his need or benefit. At this point he stole a quick glance around to see if he could detect what effect the study was having on his co-hearers, but the inscrutable faces gave little away.

Andrew quickly glanced at the clock at the side of the pulpit. "That's about an hour since we commenced," he thought. "Just about time to direct the congregation's attention to the matters for prayer."

This followed the familiar pattern that also caused Bill much genuine concern in the past. He was torn between his loyalty to and respect for Andrew and the need for radical change as he saw it, not understanding how both of these issues could be harmonized?

"Of course," Bill thought wryly, "Andrew's departure might help."

Ron had almost fallen asleep as his mind drifted to the past Saturday. His mother—he still lived at home with his parents who were not Christians—called him to the phone. A friend, Jack Kemp, was wanting Ron to attend a football game that afternoon with him. Ron had been a regular supporter of the local First Division club until he was converted, but he gradually lost the desire to attend the games. Having witnessed about the Lord to many of his old friends and having testified regarding his being saved, Ron was seldom asked to go anywhere with them now. He was puzzled why Jack should call him and it drove right out of his mind the thoughts of the paperback he had been so immersed in reading.

Ron's sleepy trance was broken as Andrew's voice brought him back to the present reality.

"Here are various matters for prayer," Andrew said, his back turned to the audience as he carefully wrote the items on a board.

"What a list!" Ron thought derisively. "I've never heard of half of these matters or persons."

"Now if any of you have other matters to add to the list, please feel free to bring them at this time," Andrew said, inclining his head slightly to the side as if expecting an avalanche of requests.

The suggestions included the needs of obscure people who were friends or distant relatives of the members, and who had various afflictions both great and small.

"My brother-in-law has been laid off," one member pleaded. "He's not a Christian, but he needs a job."

"I have been having a lot of aggravation from a very nasty workmate," one sister confided. "Please pray that God will intervene."

One bespectacled, weedy-looking young man asked in deferential tone, "Could prayer also be made for the young people that they might be blessed on their forthcoming holiday to Greece, and that the weather might be sunny for them?"

At this time Andrew said, "Let me just quickly run over

25

the items one by one."

Glancing at the clock he reminded them, "We have about 15 minutes to cover these requests, so I will open the time in introductory prayer and then you may offer your petitions."

After introductory prayer, the remaining brief period was punctuated by several prolonged moments of silence. Bill and Ron prayed, as did old Albert Higgins. He was a good soul, but he now rambled somewhat, often pausing as he searched for something else to add to his already lengthy list. Assorted general type prayers were also made for blessings on various matters before Andrew mercifully closed the prayer time. A final hymn concluded the proceedings and the congregation rapidly dispersed.

"Bill, I've been dying to see you since last weekend," Ron said excitedly.

"Oh! don't mind me," Ruth said with mock offense. "Come over to the house, or else we'll never get home to-night if you two get started talking."

Ron liked Ruth for she was very hospitable and one of the few who seemed to have a genuine interest in other members. As a result, he was no stranger to the neat villa that was the Morgan's home.

When they arrived at the Morgan home, Ruth said, "I'm going to leave you two alone because I've got quite a few things to attend to before I go to bed." She then left Bill and Ron to continue their conversation.

"Listen," Ron said, "it's unbelievable what the Lord has been doing this past week. Just wait till you hear."

Bill made allowance for the zeal of youth as he waited for Ron's revelation, but he still felt his curiosity rising.

"Right, Ron, out with it! Give me all the gory details," Bill replied somewhat sarcastically.

"Well, last Saturday morning I went down to the Christian bookstore," Ron replied. He then recounted the story of how he had acquired the paperback[5] and of his initial reservations about it.

"Do you have it with you?" Bill asked gruffly.

"Yes, right here," Ron replied, taking the grubby paperback out of his pocket.

"Hmm, not much to look at," Bill sighed.

Ron impatiently cut across his cynical remark, "Just listen to me. You know how we were discussing prayer and the state of the church prayer meetings. Well, this book is dynamite on the subject. I've read it quickly through at one go, and I'm on my second time through it because I've never read anything like it. I mean, it just shatters our concept of what prayer and prayer meetings are all about."

Bill glanced down the chapter contents of the book. *Prayer Takes in the Whole Man, Prayer and God's Work, Concerted Prayer*—these were just a few of the headings.

"Can you leave this with me?" Bill asked.

"Sure. If you promise to read it and return it to me as soon as possible," Ron answered.

"OK, all right," Bill said somewhat irritably. "I won't run away with it! By the way, does it deal with this *shopping list* business that you've been going on about so much?"

"Look, don't get me wrong," Ron responded. "I'm not very good at explanations, but I think this is what the book is saying. There is nothing wrong with a shopping list if we mean by that, specific, definite matters that we can present to our heavenly Father with a degree of certainty that we are praying according to His will and for His glory. My reading of the book suggests that there must be real unity in our asking. If I come to the church prayer meeting and casually ask the members to pray for something which burdens me greatly, but which only receives their agreement to pray about be-

27

cause I've asked them, is this the principle we read of in Matthew 18:19? I also read in a commentary[6] recently that although this statement in the context refers primarily to matters of discipline, it covers a broader spectrum when it says, 'anything that they shall ask.' I agree with these books when they assert that the Bible is not merely saying here that if two of us agree to ask anything, our Father in heaven will just send down the answers."

"So what do you believe it really means?" Bill asked Ron.

"Well, from my limited research it appears that we can think that we are agreed, but in fact we are not agreed in the manner set out in Scripture. I agree because I intensely desire it. Others in the prayer meeting agree because the shopping list requests that they pray for the item. We are not agreed as touching the matter. So we are not in harmony. We are not in real agreement in the biblical sense. I'm no expert, but I think that's the drift of what these books are saying!"

"Ron, my boy," Bill said wearily, "you've got me a bit confused. Nevertheless I think that you are on to something important here."

"Hey, it's time you guys thought about getting to your beds," Ruth called, peeking through the door.

"Yes, yes, we're just about finished," Bill replied irritably. "A couple of minutes and we'll be finished."

Ron stood up, but paused with the look of a man who had one final revelation to cap all that had gone before. "I received a phone call last Saturday from one of my friends, Jack Kemp. I used to go to football games with him, but get this, he wants to come to church with me!"

Bill was delighted because one thing they did not have in abundance in the church was young people.

They parted with a deep sense that this eventful day had

been one of special significance.

Bill was seated at his office desk the next day with a touch of the *morning blues* syndrome following the late night discussion he'd had with Ron.

"Bill Morgan," he said as he answered the phone.

"Bill, it's Andrew here. I just thought it might be good if we made it known officially to the church now, regarding my impending departure. Elaine and I have managed to tie up most of the details for moving at the end of the month."

Bill wondered if he detected a note of relief in Andrew's voice.

"Right," he said as nonchalantly as he could, "James Frame and I will discuss the best way of doing this as soon as possible."

"Thanks, Bill, I appreciate that," Andrew said as he hung up the phone.

3

The shopping list

"Wednesday evening again," Ron thought excitedly. "I must get down to the church early and share the news about Jack Kemp promising to come to the Gospel service on Sunday."

He was chatting with other members when Bill and Ruth came in, quickly followed by James Frame, and Andrew and his wife Elaine. Ron tried to speak to Bill, but before he could do so, the pastor and the two deacons disappeared quickly into the vestry.

James Frame cleared his throat nervously and addressed the other two men. Bill and he had talked the matter over, so Bill knew what was coming. Although James was many years his senior and was church secretary, he was very unsure in handling matters of church policy.

"Bill and I have discussed the situation regarding your departure, Andrew, and we feel that you should announce this just prior to the prayer time tonight. This will allow the congregation to pray for the matter right away."

At this point he looked over to Bill, uncertain of how to continue, for it had been Bill who had really framed the response to Andrew's announcement.

Bill could see James flounder and waffle a bit, so he interjected, "It'll be for the best, Andrew. After all, your heart won't really be in the work here now, and we understand that. So we'll also intimate to the church you are leaving at the end of the month with our blessing."

It seemed to Bill as he looked back across at Andrew, that the pastor was somewhat at a loss to know if he should be pleased that they had graciously accepted his resignation as tendered, or if he should be a little peeved that they had not pressed him to reconsider or at least postpone his decision.

Andrew flushed slightly as he hesitatingly said in his somewhat pompous way, "I do appreciate you men being so understanding and helpful in making my departure easier to accomplish."

* * *

The prayer meeting began in time-honored fashion. If the Holy Spirit had been at the door waiting for an entrance to the gathering, the meeting was so organized and tied to man's tradition and ordering that there was little chance He would have been invited in.[7] Several of the statements from the paperback began to run through Bill's mind and he came to the conclusion that, if the church wanted to carry on without recognition of their need of the Holy Spirit, then tragically and doubtlessly God would let them carry on by themselves."[8]

"Let us give our attention to the matters for prayer this evening, friends," Andrew said.

"I am anxious that earnest prayer would be made regarding the promise of my friend, Jack Kemp, to come to the Gospel service with me on Sunday," Ron requested.

"Yes, certainly," Andrew concurred, duly adding this item to the already extensive list of accumulated matters. "May I now beg your full attention please, as I have to bring a rather sad announcement at this time. It is with deep regret that I have to tender my resignation as pastor of Earlton Baptist Church in view of a call to Oakvale Baptist Church."

Andrew's announcement aroused a few of the dormant brigade within the congregation to a state not achievable by mentioning normal church matters. They were not aroused, however, to the point that they felt any need to pray about the matter.

Andrew was reasonably brief and to the point, and a slight buzz of subdued conversation followed his announcement.

Bill then stood and said, "As deacons, and speaking on behalf of the congregation, we are sorry that our pastor has been called to another charge. We want to wish him well, and I would like you all to join with me now in praying for God's blessing to go with him and Elaine from Earlton Baptist Church to their new ministry at Oakvale Baptist Church. I also want to suggest that in view of the immediacy of Andrew's departure, perhaps we should omit the Bible study and take a little time to pray about the move and the need of our church for a new pastor."

"Yes, of course," Andrew readily agreed.

So they inserted this item before giving attention to the shopping list.

By nature of the circumstances James Frame was making one of his rare appearances at the prayer meeting. Nevertheless, he was prevailed upon to engage in the opening prayer.

Bill groaned inwardly, "He won't come out to the prayer meetings, but we'll still be treated to a monologue of considerable length, besprinkled with clichés of antiquarian pedigree, all somehow integrated into the fabric of his prayer."

Bill knew that James would conclude his petition, irrespective of relevancy, with an unfailing reference to *Jehovah Tsidkenu.* He always seemed to find a place for this term in his intercessions. Sure enough, just as Bill thought of it, James faithfully obliged and terminated his prayer with an emphatic amen.

"Amen!" Bill said under his breath, yet with a lot more emphasis than James had uttered.

Slowly and painfully they made their way through the shopping list. Ron became furious. "We're praying here for things that should be prayed for at home," he thought angrily. "Just listen to this. 'My next door neighbor's brother-in-laws' mother has gone into the hospital to have her bunions removed.'"

Ron continued his heated line of thought. "Give me strength! None of us has ever heard of the woman.[9] And to think I have the real prospect of bringing a soul to hear the Gospel, and no one seems to care. Five minutes of prayer time left and not a mention of Jack coming on Sunday."

He was so frustrated he could not pray about his burden, consequently the meeting concluded without reference to the matter.[10] Ron could not help observing that those who burst into the loudest, most unrestrained conversation at the end of the meeting were the ones whose voices were strangely silent during the prayer time.

"How can God ever trust us with the souls of men," he thought, "when we don't even have the desire to remember them at the throne of grace?"[11]

Bill was engaged in brief parting comments with various members as he made his way to the hall exit.

Just then old Albert Higgins detained him. "Wasn't like that in our day," Albert remonstrated. "People nowadays just think they can pick up and lay down the work of God at their convenience. What do you think of this bombshell, Bill?"

Without giving Bill an opportunity to answer, Albert continued in disgruntledly fashion, "Hmm! No wonder the testimony of the Lord is held in such low esteem today."

Albert was all set to rumble on with a few more outspoken comments, lamenting particularly the lack of true spirituality, church discipline, and Christian responsibility.

"Yes, it is disturbing." Bill cut him short, but not unkindly, for he had noticed Ron looking rather sullen and downcast near the exit.

"He must be taking Andrew's leaving harder than I thought he would," Bill mused. "I must have a quick word with him."

"Hi, Ron," Bill said cheerily. "What's on your mind tonight?"

"I can not believe it, Bill," he said, shaking his head disconsolately.

"Well, it did come as a bit of a shock, but these things do happen."

"What are you talking about?" Ron said angrily, inclining his head and squinting at Bill in a half inquisitive, half remonstrative way.

Bill was taken aback. "Well, about Andrew leaving and what will—"

Ron interrupted him roughly, "For any sake, Bill, I'm not talking about Andrew."

"You're not?" Bill reacted in confusion. "Well, what on earth *are* you talking about?"

"Bill! Bill!" Ron said in exasperation. "Remember last Wednesday evening at your house?"

Bill shifted from one foot to the other uneasily.

"Bill, remember I *told* you about my friend Jack Kemp

and the possibility of him coming to the Gospel service?"

"Oh yes, of course. Is he still coming?" Bill asked in somewhat relieved tones now that his confusion had dispersed.

"I hope so, but if he doesn't, would it be any wonder?"

"I don't get it," Bill said bewilderedly.

"Tonight!" Ron said with an emphasis that startled Bill somewhat. "Tonight! The prayer meeting! I requested Andrew to pray about it, remember? But, oh no, the shopping list is so extensive, so sacred, by the time people attempt to get through it they're worn out and can't remember anything else. Can you imagine some of that stuff we supposedly prayed for, yet we omitted to mention a lost soul who has agreed to come along to the service?"

"I'll tell you what it is," Ron was getting a little heated now. "It's so long since some of them ever witnessed to a soul, never mind brought one along to the church, that they are totally out of touch!"

Bill thought that it was a bit of youthful indiscretion, but deep down he had to admit to himself that Ron had a point. Indeed, he felt convicted himself at his own lack of concern and compassion.

"Believe me," he said quietly, "I can understand now why you feel so frustrated and angry. For a start you can have my apologies for lack of interest."

Bill and Ron were last to leave the church and Ruth was already sitting in the car waiting for Bill as he locked the front door and made his way over with Ron.

"You two should take up residence here," she cried out cheerfully. "You want to come over for supper, Ron?"

"No thanks, Ruth. I appreciate it, but I've a few things I need to do before I get to bed tonight. Thanks again," he said gratefully.

Bill said quietly, "Ron, this business with Andrew and

36

all of that, I honestly believe somehow, some way, God is going to give us a new start. Even this matter you've raised tonight could be solved under Providence's purposes."

"You're right, and I'm encouraged by that thought. Let's pray that the Lord will give us a really new beginning and maybe open up things that we never anticipated. Good night, Ruth. Good night, Bill."

With these closing remarks, Ron strode off thoughtfully into the night with a degree of buoyancy that he would not have believed possible half an hour before.

* * *

As Bill turned into the driveway of their home, he said, "You know, Ruth, in spite of the upheaval and uncertainty, I honestly believe that Andrew's departure is in the will of God for Earlton Baptist Church and the work here."

"How do you come to that conclusion?" she responded.

"I'm not quite sure yet, but take my word for it. It's in my bones!" he said with a chuckle.

Bill reclined in his favorite armchair by the fireside and mulled over recent events as Ruth slipped into the kitchen to make a cup of tea.

"Yes," he thought, "all of these situations convince me that Ron is right. We have got to institute a definite program for the church in the matter of prayer. This is a priority!"

Ruth came in with a tray of tea and biscuits at this point, and thinking she had heard him speak, asked what he had said.

"I've been thinking aloud," Bill replied dreamily and in a somewhat detached kind of way.

"If ever we needed proof that we have to seriously consider the church prayer meeting, and our own private prayer

37

life, then these last few days have brought it home to me as never before!"

"I think you and Ron are hatching some plot together," Ruth said whimsically, as she sat down beside Bill.

4

They pray about everything

Alan Kerr was in his forties, of medium build, and bronzed in a way that one would expect of a man who had spent his last fifteen years in India. Alan and his wife Carol were missionaries, with two children who had been born in India.

It was a sultry day although only 7:30 a.m. The two storied house had no glass in the windows, only shutters and wrought iron grill work to keep out intruders. The house was painted in a yellow beige color which seemed so popular among Indian home owners.

Alan was seated in the front dining room, finishing breakfast with a cup of coffee and a quick look at the *Times of India*. Carol came in to ask if he wanted another cup of coffee. Without responding to his wife's inquiry, Alan said in a low voice, "Hard to imagine this is our last day here, isn't it?"

Carol felt a lump rising in her throat as she nodded in agreement. The Kerrs had made many friends in India the last fifteen years. Besides, they had helped Brother Prabaker get the church established.

"Still," Alan said reflectively, "I suppose it will be nice

to be among the folks in Earlton Baptist Church at least until we know what God has for us in the future."

"Seems a long time now since we told the old Fundamental Baptist Missionary Society that our doctrinal views had changed," Carol said with a faint smile.

"I knew they wouldn't take it too kindly," Alan replied. "But I certainly wasn't prepared for the hornet's nest it seemed to arouse back at headquarters. It was only fair, however, to inform them of the matter when we became settled in our new position."

"Yes," Carol said, "it was strange how we had never seriously considered anything so theological as the doctrines of grace before we set out for India with all our high hopes and expectations. When Stephen and Mary were born here in South India, I guess we both thought that this was to be our life work."

"Carol," Alan reflected quietly, "when I wrestled with those dawning convictions that the absolute, total sovereignty of God was taught in Scripture, I found that the effect of this truth was almost like another *born again* experience. I saw that the sovereignty of God appeared in Providence in its various ramifications, and that our births and deaths were not of the will of man, but of the will of God.[12] Again, the will of God appeared sovereign in things sacred, spiritual, and religious. Among men, God loves some and he hates some; and that before good or evil are done by them. Some are redeemed from among men by Christ, out of every kindred, tongue, people, and nation. Whom He wills and resolves to save, He saves. Others are left to perish in their sins. No other cause can be assigned to this than the sovereign will and pleasure of God.[13]"

"Hey! I'd better stop sermonizing," Alan smiled. "Anyway, remember it was just around that time when we first came home on furlough and met the folks at Earlton Baptist Church. I believe it was also then that they promised to give us a measure of support in our work."

As the two reflected on these things Alan smiled wryly, "Just shows how dangerous it is to read certain books."[14]

Carol smiled back, "But it wasn't just the books, was it, Alan?"

"No, but they certainly did drive me to the Bible to search things out. Best get a move on, Carol, we have a lot of packing to do before we leave for England."

* * *

Mrs. Shearer sat in the front room of her old-fashioned, but prim little flat. She had a cup of tea in her hand and a very perplexed look on her face.

"I just cannot believe it," she said in a mesmerized way to her friend, Martha Wood.

"Our Bethel Mission Hall closing down. I never dreamt such a thing was in the offing although it's true that numbers attending have been dwindling to nothing for some time now."

"Well, Margaret," Martha replied in a soft kindly voice, "we know that the Lord has everything under His control and it will be nice to just wait and see what He has in store for us here in Earlton now."[15] She smiled gently and reassuringly over her little gold-rimmed half spectacles, "I experienced many similar situations during my forty odd years with the China Inland Mission in many remote China provinces."

Mrs. Shearer immediately responded to her kind admonition and said, "Martha, you have been such a dear close friend to me since my husband Peter died in India. You never ever even got the opportunity to marry because of being in such isolated areas for years, but I have never heard you com-

41

plain of this once, in all our years together."

"The Lord knows all about these things," Martha responded softly.

"Yes, you're so right, Martha. How quickly we can take our eyes off the Lord when we most need to look to Him. 'I will instruct thee and teach thee in the way which thou shalt go: I will guide thee with mine eye.' That Psalm 32 was always a great encouragement to me in times of trouble and anxiety."

A holy hush fell upon the little apartment as the two precious *mothers in Israel* bowed in the presence of their God and Savior. Humility, dignity, reverence, and faith seemed compounded by the Spirit to ascend unto the living God as the fragrance of the sweetest perfume of the apothecary's art. Perfect unity prevailed[16] as the simple entreaty for divine guidance was sought concerning the closure of the Bethel Mission Hall and the need of direction as to where the two ladies would now continue to worship the Lord. They rose from their knees, but not as those who had been simply saying their prayers. Instead, they were like Hannah in the Old Testament, who "poured out her soul before the Lord."[17]

* * *

James Frame was standing in line at the Post Office on Friday morning when Bill came in with some mail to post.

"Hi, James," Bill said brightly. "Heard the news?"

"What news?" James said suspiciously. He was a little defensive because the matter of Andrew's sudden impending departure had taken them all by surprise.

"About Alan and Carol coming home," Bill continued.

"No, I certainly have not," James said in a measure relieved that it was not some other cataclysmic event that had come upon them.

"That's good news," he began. Then he quickly added, "They're all right, are they?"

"Oh, yes," Bill replied, "but you know how there has been a little uncertainty over their future for some time now. So, it looks as if they have made up their minds that the Lord wants them home again."

"Hmm, yes," James said reflectively. "That's good news for a change, eh? Must be off. See you later!"

Bill was in a studious mood as he returned to the office. His mind began to fill with possibilities that had arisen since the letter from Alan in India had come through his letter box.

"Mmm, maybe the Lord is answering quicker than we thought He would in the situation,"[18] he pondered.

"Telephone, Mr. Morgan," Alice, the office junior, broke into his thoughts insistently, causing him to reach for the phone in a reflex action.

Bill had a very busy morning, but it was Friday and he was looking forward to the weekend. He came out of the office and, entering the workshop, he saw Ron seated on a pile of carpet, eating his lunch and reading a book.

As Bill approached Ron shouted, "What a book! Did you read it all?"

"Yes, I did," Bill replied, but not as convincingly as Ron thought he should have.

"Well, what did you think of it?"

"Oh, it was excellent. In fact if you hadn't pestered me for it's return, I would have gone through it more slowly and studied it."

"Listen to this," Ron said animatedly.

Bill had no option but to stop, although he was on his way to an appointment with a customer.

"I'm in a hurry, so just read me a few lines quickly."

43

"Right!" Ron said. "Only a few lines.

> Just as it requires the whole heart given to God gladly and fully to do God's commands, so it takes the whole heart given to God gladly to do effectual praying. Because it requires the whole man to pray, praying is no easy task. Praying is far more than simply bending the knee and saying a few words by rote.[19]

"We've not even started, Bill. We've never been in a real prayer meeting. Nobody has taught us, or even considered that we might need to be taught. It's happening all over the church. Pastors, those who teach, they're all taking it for granted, most of them, that we all know how to pray."[20]

Bill nodded, "You've got a point there. Listen, excuse me. I must go or I'll be late for this appointment. We'll talk about this again at the first opportunity. Is your friend coming on Sunday evening?"

"He's promised to," Ron replied. "So I've been praying that he will come."

"Great!" Bill shouted back, as he went out through the swinging door of the workshop.

* * *

The door bell clanged noisily and Mrs. Shearer looked up from behind the counter where she had been tidying up, to see who had come into the shop.

"Well, well," she exclaimed in mock surprise, "if it isn't Mr. Morgan."

Bill smiled somewhat self-consciously, "Yes, it has been awhile since I've been in, but the pressure of work and all that—you know how it is. In fact I'm just coming back from an appointment with a customer this morning."

44

Mrs. Shearer smiled benignly and her eyes twinkled as she said warmly, "Never mind, Bill, you're always welcome."

"I just thought I'd pop in as I was passing to see if you had a nice Bible. It's Ruth's birthday next week and I noticed her old Bible is getting a bit dog-eared."

"There are quite a few here to choose from," Mrs. Shearer said. She tilted her head inquiringly and asked, "It's the Authorized Version you have, isn't it, Bill?"

"Oh yes, Ruth wouldn't have anything else and neither would I, if it came to it."

As she set out the Bibles, Bill remarked casually, "You'll have heard about Alan and Carol coming home I expect?"

"Yes," Mrs. Shearer said, "I'm so excited about it. After all, we spent time in India working quite close to one another and my husband and I met them once or twice when we were home on furlough from the mission field. I'm sure it will be a blessing for you all to have contact with them again at the church."

Bill picked up a neat calf-bound Bible. "This will suit Ruth fine. She's like me now; she needs good, clear large type to be comfortable for reading."

Bill was probing a little for an entrance to ask Mrs. Shearer's view on Andrew's departing when she spoke. "How have you taken Andrew's coming departure?" she asked, fixing her eyes upon Bill.

"Oh, er, fine," he mumbled, conscious of her gaze.

"It's the Lord's will, is it?" she pressed.

Bill felt decidedly uncomfortable for he knew that Mrs. Shearer was a truly spiritual lady. Because of this she sometimes intimidated him, though it must be said, certainly not deliberately.

Bill muttered a bit incoherently, "I suppose it is, and Andrew did feel that he had been at Earlton long enough."

He had a sinking premonition that his response had not been too satisfactory and he had an uneasy feeling that it lacked any real spiritual conviction.

Mrs. Shearer continued quietly wrapping the Bible in brown paper. She did not look up as she asked in direct fashion, "I expect that you all prayed much about such an important matter?"

It was just then that she looked straight into Bill's eyes.

"It's no use," he thought. "She knows perfectly well we never prayed about it."

But what came out of his mouth was totally different. "Well, probably not as much as we ought to have. But then Andrew seemed pretty set in his decision, so it was really up to him, I guess."

Bill was about to pick up the Bible, hand over the cash, and escape from what was becoming an embarrassing situation when Mrs. Shearer said softly, "You know, Bill, both pulpit and pew are taking these matters far too lightly in this day and age."

Bill flushed slightly as she went on, "Did Andrew have a call from God?"

Bill stammered somewhat, "Well, I suppose so. I mean that's what he said he had."

He felt a trifle more confident as he recalled, "And, there's no doubt that they wanted him at Oakvale Baptist."

His confidence that this retort would satisfy Mrs. Shearer's persistent line of inquiry was doomed to disappointment when she said, "Bill, in the thirteenth chapter of the Acts of the Apostles it says, 'As they ministered to the Lord and fasted, the Holy Ghost said, separate me Barnabus and Saul for the work whereunto I have called them.'"

Bill groaned inwardly, for he knew that this was a million miles removed from the way that James Frame, Andrew

46

or he—or indeed any of the congregation—had approached the matter. He felt crushed, yet strangely gratified because the conversation answered many of the questions that had arisen in his own heart.

Later Bill and Ruth were seated at the dining room table having their evening meal. "Listen, Ruth," Bill began emphatically. "You would not believe it. She nailed me down and I hadn't a leg to stand on. That woman has more spirituality in her little finger than we have as a whole church!" He shook his head ruefully as he continued with his meal.

"Bill," Ruth began slowly and deliberately, "it's no surprise to me that Mrs. Shearer and Martha Wood have these insights. They just live for the Lord, they pray about everything, they are careful about walking in His ways, and they know their Bibles! After all, you don't spend all the time they have on the mission field, with the kind of dedication and holiness they display, without growth in grace and understanding."

"No, you're right there," Bill replied. "But, you should have been there to hear her. She demolished my futile attempts to answer what was virtually a very simple question. I feel that the Lord is confirming that it's not merely praying that we're deficient in, but *every* aspect of the faith."

* * *

"I've been praying about it, Martha," Mrs. Shearer said to her friend as they shared a cup of coffee in the little back room of the book shop just before closing time.

"Me, too," Martha responded.

"So what do you think the Lord has for us in this situation?"

"Well, Margaret," Martha leaned forward in a confidential way, "I do believe that the Lord is impressing me to go along to Earlton Baptist Church now that the Mission Hall is closing down. I also believe that He has some little ministry there for me, even at my age."

"Martha," Mrs. Shearer said excitedly, "that's exactly what I feel the Lord has been saying to me! I've been praying about it since we got the bad news about Bethel closing down, and I'm convinced that He wants me to go to Earlton as well."

She laughed at this, with a trace of mischief in her voice, and continued, "Not that there's really much of a choice now in evangelical churches around here. Oh, it's not like the old days, is it? What with all this singing, dancing, and drama, I don't know what the church is coming to."

They agreed to get down for a season of prayer and commend the issues into God's hand before they parted company. Mrs. Shearer concluded the prayer time by saying, "Lord, thou hast taught us to 'be careful for nothing; but in everything by prayer and supplication with thanksgiving, let your requests be made known unto God.'"[21]

As she paused at the front door on her way out, Martha asked, "Is it 11 o'clock that the morning service begins at Earlton?"

"Yes. I'm sure that it is," Mrs. Shearer replied.

"Right. Then I'll see you on Sunday," Martha responded cheerfully as she strode off, remarkably sprightly for her age.

Andrew Bonar, the old Scots divine, would have approved of their prayer meeting, for he said, "God loves unity and so He loves a united cry, a petition signed by more than one."

*   *   *

The Sunday morning service had just concluded and Ron,

48

Bill and Ruth were warmly conversing with Mrs. Shearer and Martha Wood.

"Sorry to hear about the Mission Hall closing down," Bill said, "but we're delighted to have you ladies come along, and we hope that you might find a spiritual home here."

Mrs. Shearer and Miss Wood smiled benignly, "Yes, yes, we're just looking to the Lord to help us make a little contribution to the work here if it pleases Him."

Ruth interjected at this point, "Would you ladies like to come home with us and have lunch?"

"It's very kind of you, Ruth, but we have something prepared," Martha said. "But we do appreciate your very kind invitation."

Ron burst in at this point with a degree of animation as he said, "I'd really be grateful if you two sisters could remember in prayer a friend of mine who has promised to come to the Gospel service tonight. It would very much encourage me to know that you had prayed about the matter, because I know that you are able to pray so much more effectively than I can."

"Now," Mrs. Shearer said reprovingly, "Martha and I will be glad to spend a little time in prayer for this young man, but please don't think that we have any special favor with the Lord. I'm sure that your own prayers are even now commending His attention as they continue at the Throne of Grace."

"Oh, thanks so much," Ron said with some feeling. "You don't know how much it means to me, however, to have such souls as yourselves backing up my efforts to bring Jack to the church to hear the Gospel tonight."

Bill and Ruth detached themselves from the two mothers in Israel and made their way out the front door, exchanging greetings with one or two in the church parking lot before setting off home.

"What a massive privilege it will be if those two dear souls join with us here at Earlton. There just doesn't seem to be such quality saints around these days," Bill said, ruefully shaking his head.

"I'm sure that the Lord still has a remnant of choice souls, dear," Ruth said, "but I do agree that those two are something special."

5

We've never been taught to pray

Ron paced anxiously outside the church where he had arranged to meet Jack. Glancing nervously at his watch he saw that it was almost seven o'clock. "Don't tell me he's not going to come," Ron murmured. Then he reflected, "Of course it wouldn't be the first time that I've made such an arrangement only to be disappointed by fickle human nature. Still, the ladies will have prayed." This thought comforted him as he shivered slightly in the cold, damp October evening.

Ron began to let his mind drift to the subject of prayer and how dependent he suddenly seemed to be upon his feeble intercessions for the present events. "Yes, it's all right to look to the prayers of these godly ladies and hope that they get an answer, but how about my petitions?" he mused.

"It's the same story in the church," he continued to think, by now quite oblivious to the non-appearance of Jack or the bone chilling damp of the winter evening. "We all go to the prayer meeting. Some of us pray, but it's mechanical. At the end of the gathering I doubt if many could recall what we supposedly prayed about!"

Continuing in a similar vein, he began to analyze his personal attitude at this particular point. "Look at me," he

51

found himself saying almost aloud. "Am I trusting God to answer, or is all my reliance based on my own weak ability and emotions? I feel that my praying is just some type of isolated duty. It is not accompanied by other factors that I know should be present, like faith, for example." He proceeded along this line of thought as he began to make a list in his mind of things which go hand in hand with prayer.

Ron had been studying a Christian book list which catalogued several books on the subject of prayer. As he shifted impatiently from one foot to the other and anxiously scanned the gloomy, misty street for any sign of Jack, he made a mental note to order several of the books which had caught his attention. He wanted to refer to them about the essentials of prayer, a subject he had just been pondering during the wait for Jack.

It was now close to the commencement of the evening service and the last of the stragglers were emerging out of the misty gloom and slipping into the church. Dejectedly Ron was about to join them when he was startled by the sound of his friend's voice as he approached from the murky haze.

"Hi, Ron. Sorry I'm a bit late, but I got caught up in something just before I left home."

"No problem, Jack," Ron replied, trying hard to mask the delight he felt at Jack's appearing. "Let's get inside. It's freezing out here!"

Perhaps the imminent departure of Andrew from Earlton Baptist Church was weighing too heavily on his mind, but the pastor seemed more stolid and ponderous than ever in the Gospel service. Ron glanced uneasily several times at Jack, trying to assess his reaction to the message, but he could glean nothing from Jack's outward appearance.

Eventually the benediction was pronounced and the congregation filed out quickly. Andrew's last Sunday at Earlton hadn't exactly set the place on fire!

Ron felt slightly despondent as he and Jack made their way to the exit. Andrew was talking to James Frame, and everyone else seemed pre-occupied with getting home quickly on this cold damp evening.

Without anyone apparently noticing them, Ron and Jack had almost reached the front door when Martha Wood and Mrs. Shearer came out of the cloakroom and bumped into them. Ron immediately detained them with a greeting and then blurted out involuntarily, "This is Jack Kemp, ladies. Remember I told you that I'd invited him to come to church tonight?"

The two old sisters' faces were wreathed in smiles. Ron felt as if the chill of the cold wintry evening and, even worse, the chill of the reception from the uninterested members was quickly dispelled by the beaming old saints.

Martha took hold of Jack's arm lightly and said, "We're so glad to meet you, and pleased that you were able to come."

Mrs. Shearer broke in gently at this point. "And did you enjoy the service?" she asked kindly.

"Oh, er, yes," Jack stammered slightly, not knowing exactly what to say.

"I do hope that we will see you back again before long," the old saints echoed, as they slipped out into the dark, wet October drizzle.

* * *

"You're not usually home so early on a Monday night, Bill," Ruth said, when he arrived home from work somewhat unexpectedly.

"Oh, didn't you remember that we are having that special meeting tonight with the deacons and some of the men to

53

discuss the preparations for a final gathering and presentation to the Patersons before their departure later in the week?

James Frame, Nigel Smith, Albert Higgins, and a few others gathered in Bill's front room to talk about the matter. They discussed the situation, chose a suitable gift, and arranged the format of the presentation which would take place during the normal prayer meeting. The decision to forfeit a part of the prayer meeting time did not seem to cause any undue concern and the brethren were soon on their way to their various homes, satisfied about the expeditious fashion in which the matter had been concluded. But if the truth be known, the brevity of the meeting might have been related in some way to the fact that a very important European soccer match was being broadcast on TV that very evening.

* * *

On their arrival from India, Alan and Carol Kerr and their two children, Stephen and Mary, had just been picked up at Heathrow Airport by Nigel Smith. Nigel had known them as young missionary candidates before they had gone to the field.

"Kind of you to come to the airport for us, Nigel," Alan said as they made their way out of the busy terminal parking lot. "I suspect there's a lot of news we have to catch up with since we left."

"Well, actually the past few weeks have been quite hectic," Nigel replied with a degree of hesitancy, as if he wasn't sure if he should be the one to reveal the momentous events. He proceeded anyway to reveal details of the pastor's resignation and concluded by telling the Kerrs of the closing down of the Bethel Mission Hall.

"Well, well," Alan whispered softly, "there have been

some changes lately."

"Bill and Ruth would have come to meet you, but last minute business detained him," Nigel said. "However, he indicated that they would come around to see you just as soon as you have time to get settled and rested."

* * *

"I think it would be good to allow the Kerrs time to settle in after their trip from India before we visit them. Perhaps we could call on them tomorrow evening. What do you think?" Ruth asked.

"Sounds like a good idea to me," Bill replied.

On Tuesday evening, Bill and Ruth sat in the front room of the apartment which one of the church members had lent the Kerrs until they decided their future plans. After initial greetings and gleaning of much information on both sides, Bill and Alan were left alone as the ladies made supper in the kitchen.

"So, Alan," Bill said suddenly, "what do you make of it all?"

"About Andrew, you mean?"

"Yes," said Bill, with a touch of uncertainty in his voice. "You know that he is going off at the end of the week and we postponed doing anything about getting anyone to deputize, when we knew that you were coming home. What I'm really saying is that I've discussed it with the other deacon and the men, and they agree with me that it seems providential that you have come home just at this critical time. We wondered if you could fill the pulpit for us temporarily until we find our feet?"

"Well, I, er, I'm not really sure," Alan stuttered, a little taken aback by the directness of Bill's approach. "I don't even know Andrew Paterson, and he might not be happy at such an arrangement."

Bill cut in quite bluntly, "Look, Alan, it's nothing to do with Andrew now. If it's money or anything that's the problem, we can afford to give you the stipend that Andrew had, and no doubt this will help you until you establish what God wants you to do."

"Bill, it's not money or anything like that. It's just knowing if this is God's plan for us right now. But, I'll tell you what, I realize that the church is in a bit of a dilemma right now. So let's put it this way, I'll be glad to help out in any way I can until you all have time to get things sorted out."

"Great," Bill said enthusiastically, just as the ladies came in with sandwiches and a pot of tea.

"You two seem pleased with yourselves," Carol said inquiringly. The men nodded at her statement, but left it there, as they began to engage in more general conversation.

* * *

It was Wednesday lunch time when Ron decided to slip down to the Christian book shop to have a chat with Mrs. Shearer and inquire if she had uncovered any other books on the subject of prayer. In truth, Ron was also keen to know if Mrs. Shearer and Miss Wood had been continuing to pray after Jack Kemp's visit to the church the past Sunday night.

Ron swung breezily through the front door of the little shop and found Mrs. Shearer behind the counter checking paper work.

"Hello, Ron," she said cheerfully, as was her custom. "Is that your lunch you have with you? Let me put the kettle on and we'll eat together."

"Thanks a lot," Ron responded gladly, but he wasn't

surprised at her invitation because she was always hospitable to everyone she met.

They settled down in the small back room and Ron, eager to speak to her about Jack's visit, dispensed with the preliminaries and quickly said, "What did you think about Jack's response to the service?"

"Oh it's early days yet," she replied quietly, "but Martha and I have committed it all to the Lord and prayed for his salvation."

"That's great," Ron said, his face lighting up with pleasure. "I've been praying, too, and trying to exercise faith that Jack will repent and be saved."

"By the way," he continued, "you haven't come across any more books on prayer for me have you?"

"Well, after your reaction to the first one, I have picked up another two paperbacks by E. M. Bounds which I thought might interest you."

"Terrific!" Ron exclaimed. "Just tell me how much I owe you. You can be sure I'll be giving them a good reading and careful study."

"That's all right," she said. "Just one little point though. There are many more good books on prayer, but I think Bounds is good for whetting the appetite."

Ron was leaning back in his chair and finishing a mug of tea when he changed the subject and said, "Mrs. Shearer, isn't it wonderful about the Kerrs coming home, especially at this time."

Mrs. Shearer nodded gently, "Ron, the Lord is so good. Sometimes He answers our prayers even before we ask Him. I'm sure whatever the ultimate outcome is, Alan will be a tremendous help to the church just now."

"Do you think he might even become the pastor?" Ron blurted out excitedly.

Mrs. Shearer smiled benignly, "Now, Ron, let's not run ahead of the Lord's purposes. God will show us His mind in due season if we wait on Him."

"Oh, ah, yes, of course," Ron stammered. "I just thought it would be wonderful if the Lord were going to solve our problems quickly."

Mrs. Shearer shook her head in a motherly fashion as Ron disappeared through the front door, clutching the books in his hand.

As soon as Ron arrived home, he sat down and examined the books that he had picked up from Mrs. Shearer. The first was obviously a twin of the book he already had. This one was entitled, *The Necessity of Prayer*.[22] The other caught his attention because it was not a paperback as he had first thought, but a slim hardback called, *Power Through Prayer*.[23]

Ron casually flicked through the pages of the paperback and his attention was arrested by the statement, "Prayer without fervor, stakes nothing on the issue, because it has nothing to stake, it comes with empty hands."[24]

"Fervency," Ron deliberated. "What does it really mean? Now if I go to the local soccer match and it's an important game, I certainly see fervor there. There's heart and heat in it all. I've never been in a prayer meeting with these qualities. Let me try and note several essentials for real praying." He reached for his Bible and a sheet of writing paper and began to list various statements.

Ron looked over his list with a bewildered unbelief. "It's just what I was saying to Bill in the workshop a few days ago. We've never been taught to pray."

He continued thinking aloud, "Andrew hardly ever mentioned the word, far less instructed any of us. And, regarding it being God's will—well, we just seemed to assume that it was."

He quickly looked down the list he had made and thought, "This is confusing. Either I'm stupid or I have been missing something important up till now. Most of us in the church are in the same boat I guess, except . . . " He paused as the thought gripped him, "Except Mrs. Shearer and Miss Wood."

Ron reluctantly closed his Bible and laid down his pen. "Well," he pondered deeply, "I wonder if Alan will be able to help me with these difficulties?" With this thought lingering in his mind he realized that it was time he was leaving for the prayer meeting if he was to avoid being late.

6

Prayer is the heart of the church

Bill arrived at the church early before the prayer meeting was due to begin. He had arranged to meet in the vestry for a while with several of the men and Alan before the meeting. Soon, Nigel Smith, Albert Higgins, and James Frame joined Bill in waiting for Alan's arrival.

James seemed slightly edgy and unsettled. "But then," Bill thought to himself, "he's not used to attending the Wednesday night prayer meeting."

Just then Alan came in and warm handshakes were exchanged all round. Bill was the spokesman for the deacons and he expressed an affectionate welcome to Alan and his family on their return to the church from India.

Bill, addressing Alan directly, said, "Alan, we're delighted as deacons and congregation to welcome you back and to say that in appreciation of your stepping in to help us in our present difficulty, we want you to feel free to act and carry out your duties as the Lord leads."

A murmur of approval emanated from the others, and after a brief word of prayer, they adjourned to the church where a fair number of the members had already gathered.

"It is my great pleasure and honor to welcome the Kerr

family back into our midst and to introduce them to any who have not had the opportunity to meet them before." Bill continued to address the congregation saying, "We as deacons also want to acknowledge our gratitude to Alan who has agreed to minister to us and take up pastoral duties in the interim period."

Alan responded, "I wish to thank the deacons and congregation for giving me the privilege to assume the important office of pastor as we prayerfully seek someone to take over the office in the days ahead."

With the preliminaries over, the meeting followed the usual pattern except that Alan shared something of the work in India which had occupied them over the past years. He had also decided that he would adopt a low-key attitude at first until he found out the strengths and weaknesses of the church. It had been a long time since he had last attended any meetings at Earlton Baptist Church, and he therefore was out of touch with its spiritual life and condition.

"Could we utilize the time remaining to pray and seek God's face?" Alan asked. "Bill, would you be good enough to lead us in a little season of prayer?"

He had asked Bill if he would lead the prayer time so that he could get the feel of things, and Bill was happy to do so. Ron was impatient for Alan to take over leadership, but realized that he did require some time to adjust to the situation. So he settled in his mind that things would follow the normal procedure for this evening at least.

Bill cleared his throat as he stood before the gathering, "If any of you friends have any prayer requests or would like to share regarding God's goodness to you during the past week, then please take the opportunity."

One lady rose near the back of the hall and said, "I have been praying that my nephew would get a job, as he has been unemployed for six months, and the Lord has marvelously answered by granting him an interview next week. Can we pray that it will be successful?"

"Yes, certainly," Bill mumbled a little shamefacedly.

"Oh, could I bring a request here?" asked another lady of substantial proportions who was dressed, Bill noticed with some distaste, in a purple suit and who apparently desired not to be outdone.

"My grandmother, who is not a Christian, slipped getting out of bed yesterday and hurt her hip. She is in a retirement home where they look after her very well, but I would like us to pray that the Lord would speak to her soul through this accident."

This was all solemnly noted by Bill as he asked, "Is there anything else we should remember?"

Old Albert rose at this, though somewhat unsteadily. Adopting a ministerial pose, with his half spectacles perched on the end of his nose, he announced, "The Lord has been speaking to me and I want to share this concern with the church."

Rustling to and fro through his Bible, he eventually found the passage in Habakkuk 3:2 that had so impressed him.

Ron thought, "Here we go again. Is this the only verse that God has ever spoken to him about?"

Sure enough, Albert began to wax eloquently on the terrible need of revival, interspersing anecdotes acquired over the years concerning the Welsh revival. The shuffling of feet and nervous coughing of several members were apparently lost on Albert, and Ron fumed inwardly long before Albert mercifully drew to a halt.

Ron glanced at Alan, but he gave no indication of how he was reacting. Turning his eyes to the other side of the hall, Ron saw the godly old sisters, Mrs. Shearer and Miss Wood, but he was disappointed to see they looked as benign as ever.

"I would like to ask for prayer for Jack Kemp," Ron found himself saying almost before he realized it. This was also duly noted by Bill, who then suggested that they should pray. The requests and preliminaries had taken almost half an hour, so there was only about quarter of an hour left for actual intercession.

Bill opened with an introductory prayer mentioning most of the items requested. A lengthy lapse of time followed before Mrs. Smith ventured to pray for something not on the shopping list. This was concerning the Sunday School work. It was a rather disjointed utterance, punctuated by stoppages which suggested that she was about to conclude, but which unfortunately were only preludes to further meandering. Finally and thankfully, she ended.

Ron could contain himself no longer when he realized the prayer time was ending and no one seemed to be interested enough to pray for Jack Kemp. He burst forth with an impassioned eruption of youthful zeal, fueled by his frustration at the seemingly aimless vain repetitions and lukewarm attitudes. His voice rose to a crescendo, as he unconsciously and obliquely, began to scold the assembled gathering.

"How can we expect you, Lord, to bring people into this church when we have such a lack of interest in lost souls and visitors? I believe that you have specifically brought souls in, and we have failed to be grateful to you or genuinely interested in them."

In a somewhat jerky, unsure fashion, Bill nervously took the first opportunity to close the meeting. It was almost as if he were looking over his shoulder to see if there would be another heated outburst that might sweep him away in a frenzy of uncertainty. Gratefully he reached the haven of his final amen without further assault and with a measure of relief.

* * *

Carol Kerr quizzed Alan at the breakfast table, "What did you make of the meeting last night?"

"Well," he responded slowly and thoughtfully, "it makes me wish I had been a little more reticent in accepting the task of leading the church in this interim period."

"Pretty lifeless kind of a prayer meeting," Carol said despondently.

"It's a definite challenge," Alan said reflectively, "and to tell you the truth, I'm not sure I'm up to it anymore."

Carol laughed cheerfully as she made her way into the kitchen. "I don't think you're ready to be put out to pasture yet," she called over her shoulder.

"You know," Alan continued, "I feel sorry for that young Ron. I mean, I know that he preached to us all, but he had a valid point. He was the only one who seemed to have anything resembling a real heart burden in his cry. Most of the others, sadly, are spiritual icebergs. The Spirit of God is going to have to melt them!"

* * *

It was Thursday morning and Mrs. Shearer and Martha Wood were having a cup of coffee in the back room of the little Christian book shop. "Oh, Martha," Mrs. Shearer sighed deeply, "truly prayer is the very heart of any church."

"Yes, yes," Martha nodded in agreement, "we have to pray for Alan. The devil is going to make his task very difficult. If Alan tries to get the prayer meeting into shape, then he is certainly going to be a target for the enemy."

"It saddens me to have to say so," Mrs. Shearer said

65

wistfully as she began to clear the coffee cups from the table, "but the prayer meeting has been allowed to exist without instruction, cultivation, or direction until it has reached its present moribund state. I do pray the Lord will use Brother Alan to instruct and lead and remind us of our dire need of the spirit of grace and supplication being poured upon us." [25]

"Oh, where will any man begin his labors to bring a proper sense of propriety, dignity, awe, and sensitivity to this situation?" Martha looked forlornly at Mrs. Shearer as she posed her question.

"Well, dear," Mrs. Shearer replied kindly, "the Lord knows, but I have to say that I fear there is trouble on the horizon."

The two old saints got down on their knees beside the worn sofa and began to seek the Lord about the matter, breathing out supplications in a way that was unknown in the church prayer meetings.

7

This is the kind of preaching we need

Alan Kerr was seated at his desk in the vestry when he heard the church door open and footsteps approaching. There was a light tap on the vestry door and he responded, "Come in!"

Ron entered, looking a little sheepish, and immediately apologized for disturbing Alan's study time.

"No, no, not at all," Alan said warmly.

"You're Ron Coltart?" Alan asked, apologizing that he had not had sufficient time to learn the names of all those who had joined the congregation during his long absence.

"Yes, that's right," Ron replied. "I have some time to spare at my lunch hour, and I just thought I would drop in and have a chat if it's not causing you any inconvenience."

"No. Glad to see you," Alan said. "I'm really quite eager to get to know all the folks in the church, particularly as I've been thrown in at the deep end, as it were, till a pastor is appointed."

They chatted on and off about various things, but Alan sensed that Ron had something on his mind other than all the social niceties of the moment.

Just then Ron looked directly at Alan and said, "I kind

of wanted advice and the opportunity to express concern for a matter that has bothered me for a while."

"Sure, go ahead," Alan said as he leaned back in his chair. Ron had the uneasy feeling that Alan could read what was on his mind, nevertheless he began to unfold his unease over the matter of prayer in his own life and in the church prayer meetings.

"Look, Mr. Kerr," he began.

"Just call me Alan," the interim pastor interjected in a gracious way that allayed Ron's fears.

"Oh, er, thanks, Alan," Ron sputtered. "It's just that, well, I recognize that I'm something of a novice in spiritual matters. But I have been discussing this issue with my boss, Bill Morgan, and I've also mentioned it to the two sisters at the book shop."

"What's on your mind then?" Alan asked, leaning forward a little as if he had an unusual degree of curiosity and anticipation concerning what Ron was about to say.

"You see," Ron started somewhat hesitantly, "it all began a couple of months ago when Mrs. Shearer gave me a book on prayer by E. M. Bounds. I couldn't help comparing the things he was saying with my own feeble efforts in prayer and also the state of our church prayer meeting. I hope that you don't think it is pride or arrogance on my part to be thinking along these lines?"

Alan sighed deeply. Resting his chin on his hand, he looked at Ron as though searching for the right words. He nodded first, then said quietly, "You know, Ron, I'm very encouraged and delighted when I hear of young people particularly having desire to read literature by E. M. Bounds and other godly men of like mind. However, just a word of caution, if I may. It can be a very tricky matter seeking to implement the principles set forth in such books, and it requires delicate handling. In view of this, we have to be careful that our sense of frustration at times does not overrule our discretion. By the way, I'm hoping to address these issues in forthcoming prayer meetings. I'm encouraged that it appears I'll have one person at least who will be sympathetic to my thoughts on the subject." Alan continued, "I know we don't have a lot of time right now, but maybe you would like to outline your concerns, and if I can help, I'll certainly be glad to do so."

"Thanks," Ron began. "I've discussed this a bit with Bill and I know that he's also concerned about these things. I wrote a few items down and if you could consider them and give me your opinion on them, not necessarily right now, I'd be really grateful." Ron took a grubby scrap of paper out of his inside jacket pocket and, smoothing out its wrinkled surface, read the contents.

"First . . ." he cleared his throat nervously. "First, Bounds emphasizes the necessity of prayers having to do with the whole man.[26] He goes on to say that men must be entirely given over to God in prayer. They should not be double-minded, should not vacillate. They should be holy, and they should have undivided faith and the energy of fire."

Ron stopped there and looked appealingly and straight at Alan. "I'm the opposite of this!" he said despairingly. "And I have not heard anything remotely resembling this in our church prayer meeting either! But what really worries me is that nobody seems alarmed about it."

Alan said consolingly, "That's a pretty dismal picture you are painting, Ron."

In his mind, however, he thought, "This lad is not far off the target in his assessment of that prayer meeting."

Ron interrupted Alan's brief moment of reverie as he exclaimed, "The old sisters are not like that though, Alan!"

He paused, and with a little difficulty expressing what he felt, continued disjointedly. He felt that he might be considered something of a traitor because of his revelations of what he considered grave omissions in the church.

"I'm sorry if I sound critical," he said sincerely. "I know that I'm inexperienced and sadly lacking in these areas myself. I also realize that I might well be accused of being carried away by reading a couple of books, but I'm convinced that the Bible substantiates the emphasis of the books. What do you think, Alan?"

"Well," Alan said pensively as he looked at Ron, "I agree in the main with your sentiments, but there is something that I would like you to do for me."

"Sure!" Ron said quickly. "What's that?"

"This is a serious issue and requires much wisdom, tact, and patience," Alan said slowly and thoughtfully. "I want you to diligently show me that these are not just cheap words that you have repeated to me this morning. So, will you begin to pray that God will help me and all who are concerned about such matters to address them and see them changed in the days ahead?"

"Right!" Ron said brightly. "You can count on me, Alan."

Ron's lunch hour had rapidly concluded and the grubby scrap of paper with his list of questions was returned to his pocket, the majority of the questions still not discussed.

After Ron left the vestry, Alan continued staring ahead for a long time as his mind filled with recollections, forebodings, and some fears, mingled with a touch of excitement. These arose as he thought of what lay in front of him and the challenge that was now emerging.

"Hmm!" he grunted to himself, "and I'm not even the official pastor!"

* * *

James Frame and his wife Jean were having, if not a heated discussion, certainly an animated one as they sat at their evening meal on Wednesday.

"Listen, Jean, you know that it's not convenient for me to go to church on Wednesdays and, if I start to go now, well, it will set a precedent and people will just expect me to be there all the time."

"But, James," Jean said sympathetically, "I know that you are a busy man and so do the church folks. But as Alan Kerr is going to be leading the meeting alone for the first time since pastor left, and with you being the church secretary, I think it would be good if you went along tonight anyway. You don't have to make a habit of it, only just for this occasion."

"Oh, all right," James replied with irritation. "But don't expect me to be there every Wednesday!"

There was a better than average attendance at the first prayer meeting which Alan was to conduct. James Frame and his wife were seated in the back row looking decidedly uncomfortable as they surveyed the congregation. The two godly old sisters were seated near the front with Ron beside them. Ruth and Bill were just behind, looking quite expectant as they awaited Alan's announcement of the first hymn.

Alan pared down the preliminaries and more than a few present appeared apprehensive when they looked at the clock and realized that he had taken only 15 minutes to cover the notices, a chore that usually took at least 40 minutes or so. Several sensed ominously that it was going to be a long hard night.

"Will you please open your Bibles to James 4 as we read the first three verses," Alan told the congregation. "Because of time limitations, we will focus on verse three. I want to emphasize to you as believers the crucial nature of prayer in the life of a Christian and a church. What a tragedy it is when people come together to pray and to receive answers from heaven, and their praying rises no higher than the ceiling because they totally ignore God's terms and conditions for answers."[27]

"Praying," Alan continued, "can be nothing more than a hindrance, rather than a blessing, if engaged upon without recognition of certain essential elements. Have you ever considered the ground rules?"

Alan challenged the saints as he warmed to his theme, but signs of unease were surfacing, particularly with James Frame and several older members.

"Motive is the first consideration," Alan went on, "for it is very possible to be praying for a proper thing in the wrong way."

James Frame's head was down at this point, dark thoughts scurrying through his mind, not the least that he wished he had never come to the meeting.

"I cannot underline too strongly," Alan continued, "how good a thing it is to pray for the increase of souls to be added to the church. However, it is not a good thing, if the main reason is to have a bigger church and more prestige thereby. If the possibility of survival through increased financial support because of greater numbers is a leading factor, then this constitutes wrongly directed praying. It is far removed from the primary objective of the glory of God."

At this point Alan apologized for taking more time than he had intended, so he told the congregation he would leave the matter there in the meantime and they could turn to prayer.

Those in the meeting who were under the delusion that the recitation of the shopping list would give them space to recover their composure and kill off most of the remaining time were to be sadly disillusioned.

Alan said very briefly, "Friends, we have enough to pray over this evening in the light of the challenge posed by this one scripture, James 4:3. So, let us concentrate in asking the Lord to begin to teach us how to pray in a manner pleasing in His sight and to examine our motives in His holy presence."

After Alan had briefly committed the time to God and had asked for His enablement by the Spirit, a deathly silence followed. Just as the silence became almost totally embarrassing, the quiet sweet tones of Mrs. Shearer's voice relieved the anxiety of one or two of the more concerned souls.

"Lord," she said with her accustomed awe and reverence, "thou knowest how grateful we are that your voice was heard in our gathering tonight. What manner of people would we be if we sought not to thank thee for such kindness in bestowing this blessing upon us. Help us to carry the savor and import of this challenge as we leave this place, and to ponder thy servant's words to our edification, spiritual advancement, and your glory."

At this point, Ron felt motivated to charge into the arena and pray in a loud and emotional fashion for Jack Kemp.

James Frame was greatly startled and unnerved by the young zealot's sudden exclamation. He and others of similar ilk grimaced inwardly and glanced again at the clock which seemed to be making interminably slow progress toward the normal closing time.

* * *

James Frame managed conveniently to exit the church alongside Roger Drury. Roger was something of a malcontent in the church since he had been passed over several times in the election of deacons.

"Now then, Roger," James said confidentially and out of the corner of his mouth, "what do you make of this tonight?"

Roger, never slow to assert his opinions, retorted strongly, "All I can say is that I'm glad that he . . ." Roger heavily emphasized the *he* in sarcastic fashion. "I'm certainly glad that *he* is not the pastor for if he were, then I for one would not be around here."

He finished his statement with a nod that brooked no denial and which found mutual response in James Frame's heart.

Just as they were about to go their way James said casually, "Maybe you and Celia would like to come around some evening for a chat?"

"Yes, we certainly would," Roger replied.

Having made suitable arrangements to visit, they made their way from what had been a very eventful meeting for all concerned.

Bill Morgan and Ruth were also conversing with Ron, Mrs. Shearer, Miss Wood, the Kerrs, and another young couple, Tim and Sally Robson. Tim was a teacher and his wife Sally was a nurse, though she was not working now because they had a recently had a baby daughter. The Robsons had been saved about three years and appeared to be very faithful Christians. Bill offered to carry the elderly ladies home. Though they protested that they could easily walk, Bill insisted and ushered them into his car. Alan and Carol wished them all goodnight and headed down the street to their flat.

* * *

As they relaxed with a cup of tea at home, Carol broached

74

the subject of the prayer meeting.

"How do you think it went?" she inquired with a puzzled look on her face.

"You're saying that as if you had some doubts," Alan parried.

"Well, call it woman's intuition if you like, but I detected ripples beneath the surface and I would not be surprised if there were some opposition to the upsetting of the status quo."

"Carol," Alan said in a slightly exasperated manner, "I'm not upsetting the status quo! I'm trying to bring a biblical perspective to the meeting, and I intend to do it gradually over the coming weeks."

"Uh huh, if you get the time to do it," Carol said with the frankness that characterized her attitude and which Alan often found both endearing and disturbing.

Upon arriving home, Mrs. Shearer pressed the Morgans, Ron, and Martha to come in and have supper together. The bright-eyed, cheery invitation was too much to resist. So they all went into the little apartment behind the book shop and were soon settled comfortably.

Ron's youthful zeal knew no abating. Soon he was posing the question as to what the others thought of the prayer meeting.

"I really felt that Alan laid it out clearly and brought a great message," Ron said excitedly. "This is the kind of preaching that we need to hear if things are to be changed."

With a bit of hesitation Bill said quietly, "The message certainly made you think, and I suppose it shows how far we, as a church and as individuals, are from true biblical praying."

After everyone bowed their head, Bill gave thanks for the food before them. Then Martha Wood glanced up as if looking for approval from her friend Mrs. Shearer, and finally began to say in a soft voice, "Margaret and I have been concerned about issues in the church and we have made it a matter of prayer for God's help and wisdom for Brother Alan as he begins to lead the church at this time. But we all need to realize that Brother Alan is going to have a most difficult task and he will need much prayer support."

"However," she continued seriously, "let us not expect miracles from Alan. We must give the Holy Spirit His place and beseech Him that the congregation might be wrought upon so that they begin to pray in a spontaneous, fervent, and earnest manner."[28]

A brief silence followed Miss Wood's pronouncement before Mrs. Shearer, surveying them all with a kindly eye, said in a hushed voice, "Friends, we do need to be careful as Alan begins this daunting task. We must ask God to make the people's minds receptive. As hopefully the truth grips their understanding, then we must pray it down into their hearts! We don't want men to be convinced of the truth of Scripture in their minds alone."

"I have just been reading, *Knowing the Times*[29] by Dr. Martyn Lloyd Jones." At this she pulled the volume out of a drawer in the table. "See here in the eleventh chapter he says,

> Lastly, let us realize that the weapons of our warfare are not carnal, but mighty through God, powerful in the power of God. Let us realize that we can be orthodox, yet dead. Let us realize that we can be highly intellectual and theological, yet dead."

Ron reached out for the volume and mentally made a note to get a copy as soon as possible.

"Oh, for a breath of God in the midst," Mrs. Shearer said emotionally with eyes half closed. "For without Him we can do nothing."[30]

8

We cannot lose in the praying business

Ron could not believe his eyes! It was the conclusion of the Sunday evening Gospel service and Jack Kemp was accompanying Alan Kerr to the church vestry. The preacher had invited anyone who wanted to discuss any of the matters raised in the sermon or who had any questions regarding how they might become a Christian. Alan had preached from Romans 3:22:23, "For there is no difference: for all have sinned, and come short of the glory of God."

James Frame, Roger Drury, and old Albert Higgins were leaving the church together with several of the less committed members. The Morgans and the two old sisters from the book shop congregated around Ron and waited expectantly for Jack to emerge from the vestry. It wasn't long before he and Alan came out and the smile on his face told the whole story.

"I've been saved tonight," Jack blurted out. Somewhat at a loss for words, he looked around the little group for inspiration on how to continue. He was soon surrounded by all of them shaking his hand and the elderly sisters giving him motherly hugs.

This joyous little scene went unnoticed by the band of

regulars who had slipped out earlier, intent only in making it home without delay.

* * *

Ron had been quick to counsel Jack to attend all the meetings now that he was a Christian, and Jack was sitting beside him as they waited for the Wednesday night prayer and Bible study to begin. James Frame was also in attendance and seated on the back row with the Drurys and other back seat residents of long standing. His attendance was not prompted by a spiritual reawakening, but rather so he could "keep an eye on things," as he had told Roger Drury.

Alan began the prayer meeting in the radical new style that was not going down too well with the traditionalists. After the opening hymn and a reasonably brief public prayer, he turned to the announcements. These had previously been the highlight for many members as they covered matters minuscule, irrelevant, and unimportant, interspersed with a few basic necessities. All this did, however, cut down the time allotted for prayer and this was satisfactory to the back row brigade. If one then added the sacrosanct shopping list to the proceedings, one could reckon on 40 minutes being filched from the time generally allowed for prayer. Alan had wielded a Gospel machete on these practices so that the schedule allowed 10 minutes for preliminaries, 30 minutes for ministry, and nearly an hour for prayer.

Alan was not so much concerned with homiletical excellence as serious exhortation. "Just a verse for us to consider for a moment or two before we come to prayer," he said.

He was acutely aware of the undercurrent of opposition emanating from certain parties in the church at this supposed flagrant usurping of the *status quo* in the order of service.

"Well," he consoled himself inwardly, "at least I haven't been hired so I can't be fired!"

"Please turn to Matthew 18:19," he heard himself saying as the sullen professors' hostility seemed to insidiously advance upon him from the region of the back row brigade and their supporters. "Agreement, unity—these are vital necessities if the church is going to get its prayers answered."

Alan looked out and saw that a few were hanging on to his words while others were visibly uneasy. He continued, "There are pre-conditions for receiving answers to prayer, and I believe the Christian populace generally are untaught in this matter. Perhaps we have to concede that pastors may be partly responsible for this by seldom, if ever, addressing the question of teaching people to pray. I am going to suggest to you that the majority of prayers made to God by Christian people, individually or corporately, do not meet the biblical requirements in many areas. It is not sufficient that we merely turn up for a meeting. That is good as far as it goes. But how did we prepare ourselves to come? Is prayer a duty to be endured rather than a privilege to be embraced? Do we come into the house of prayer as if it were some club or social gathering? Do we chatter away noisily about this and that and then expect God to immediately tune in to our many requests that so often just come into our heads on the spur of the moment? If we have no burden or concern as to whether our prayers are in harmony with God's will and the mind of our fellow saints, what shall we say of unity and harmony?"

"Let's put it like this. Look at Matthew 18:19: 'That if two of you shall agree on earth as touching anything that they shall ask, it shall be done for them of my Father in heaven.' Agreement and unity are vital indispensable ingredients for praying that will move the heart of God."

79

"I believe . . ." Alan said slowly and deliberately, "I believe that we would probably find this congregation is not even agreed on the reasons or motives for coming to church tonight, far less than having agreement on unified objectives in prayer."

This all came as a calamitous blow to James Frame and his cronies. Slowly shaking his head, he fidgeted and looked over at his supporters. Alan saw this out of the corner of his eye and, though discouraged and disappointed, continued to press home his theme.

"A lack of regard for the means instituted by God for the furtherance of His kingdom is inexcusable. A slovenly approach and lack of preparation in coming to the house of God and little sense of reverence when we finally arrive here, are not calculated to be pleasing to the Almighty nor to persuade Him to answer our petitions. To be absolutely honest we may have to admit that these iniquities have separated us and our God. "[31]

Alan paused just before he concluded. The atmosphere was electric and one could almost feel the static in the air!

"Friends," he exclaimed with impassioned plea, "we must begin to rectify these matters before we can hope for a revival in our midst."

Alan knew that he had been pressing matters strongly, even overstating the case so he could bring a powerful correction to years of indifference and ignorance. It was a calculated risk, but he had prayed about it and had weighed the issues as comprehensively as he could. He had decided that the risk would be worthwhile. After all, he had no guarantee of any lengthy time to effect the changes he felt crucially needed to be made.

"And," he sadly reflected, "personal prayer and church prayer meetings seem to be at a very low ebb nationwide.

There cannot be many experts on the subject or things would be different. I'm certainly no expert myself, but by God's grace I'm going to attempt to get some kind of viability and God-honoring exercise into this prayer meeting."

"I won't detain you longer," Alan said. "In view of what we have been saying this evening, however, it would now be good to bring these matters before God. First, we should praise Him and give thanks that He still bears with us. Second, with heartfelt intercession we must pray that He might teach us *how to pray*. Third, we must offer sincere prayer for lost souls. Finally, we must pray concerning our great need of a pastor."

"I think if we cover these items earnestly and in unity we will have accomplished something of eternal value tonight," Alan concluded. "Let us pray."

As he got down on his knees he was conscious that about half of those present joined him while others shuffled nervously, unsure what to do.[32]

"Now you older folks, or any who have ailments that prevent you kneeling with us, don't worry. Just pray where you are," Alan called out, lest any should feel that they must unquestionably comply with his directive.

James Frame and Roger Drury had slipped out of the hall just as the prayer time began. Alan wasn't conscious of their going although Ron and Bill, among others, had heard them depart.

The disgruntled group met outside the church entrance and quickly decided to go to James Frame's home to discuss the evening's events. James and Roger led the way with Jean and Monica, Roger's wife, bringing up the rear. Another couple, Phil and Gwen Wilson, had been sitting near the Frames and were almost swept aside by them as they stormed out of the church. They joined the exodus anyway because Gwen was friendly with Jean Frame.

It was no coincidence that Gwen was also the dominant partner in her marriage.

They all quickly settled with coffee and biscuits and began agitatedly to air their complaints and grievances.

"I think it's ridiculous that this man should try and disrupt our church services when he's only been back here at the church for a few weeks." Gwen Wilson's bellicose tones indicated what she thought of the proceedings, although the effort she had made seemed to make her look even more frail than she was.

"Yes, you're right, Gwen," said James Frame, fawning in a manner which he had no doubt cultivated during his many years of seeking promotion by political strategies on his Civil Service job.

"It just isn't good enough!" Roger exploded in a red faced outburst. "Who the he . . ." He paused momentarily, reigning in the expletive that he was about to articulate. "Who the dickens does he think he is anyway?"

Jean Frame retorted, "Something will have to be done about it." She nodded to the heated group in what she thought was a sagacious manner.

"Yes, dear," James said quietly, now seeking to calm down the atmosphere a little. "I think we should propose an extraordinary business meeting to discuss the whole matter." He looked over his half spectacles with a hard beady eye, inviting approval for his suggestion.

"Not before time," Roger grunted, "or we'll find the church taken out of our hands before we know it!"

The proposal met with general approval from the others and it was left to James Frame to canvass members to gauge support for their scheme.

* * *

82

Alan and Carol had invited the Morgans and Jack and Ron to their house for supper after the service. They had also invited Nigel and Marjorie Smith, but the Smiths thanked them and declined, saying they really needed to get the girls home before it was too late.

Ruth went into the kitchen to help Carol prepare supper while the men seated themselves comfortably in the front room.

Ron quickly got into his stride. "That was a tremendous time tonight, Alan. You made it crystal clear what we have to do if we are to make any decent progress in prayer."

He looked piercingly at Bill, almost hypnotizing him into making comment.

Bill moved uneasily in his chair as he murmured, "Er, yes, I believe it was a very profitable time we had tonight."

In turmoil and apprehensive about what might lie ahead, Bill cleared this throat and paused. Trying to be diplomatic, he painstakingly searched for the right words. He felt sure that what Alan had said was right and needful, but he wasn't sure about his own resolution to see the matter through to its ultimate conclusion.

Suddenly he found himself saying, "Eh, yes, things are in a bad state and this does require drastic action. We need God's help and guidance because I feel that trouble is brewing."

At this point Alan said reflectively, "We can take it for granted that the devil will certainly not allow us to proceed unopposed if there is the possibility of spiritual advance in what we seek to do. Let's just take a moment to ask God for wisdom and help right now." So they bowed their heads in prayer.

When they had finished praying, Bill said nervously,

"Look, Alan, please don't misunderstand me when I say that I feel that trouble is brewing. I suppose I'm basically the sort of person who likes a quiet life and seeks to avoid trouble at all costs."

"I suppose most sensible people feel like that," Alan said with a wry smile, "but, look at it this way, is any instructed Christian going to be surprised when trouble confronts him? 'Man that is born of woman is of few days and full of trouble.'[33] Now the Lord knows that none of us here is out looking for trouble. All of us would concur with your sentiments in this respect."

Alan looked around the company at this point and saw that they were all listening intently. Bill leaned forward slightly, head cocked to one side. Ruth sat next to him, and although her countenance revealed a degree of anxiety, she was paying rapt attention to Alan's words. Ron's attitude was different. He had the light of battle in his eyes and a desire, kindled by the impetuosity of youth, to charge into the fray with wild abandon.

Alan continued in measured tones, "If there is going to be trouble in our lives, then you can be assured it will arise when we begin to get serious about prayer. But there are benefits even here. When trouble arrives as we begin to pray, this can be utilized to motivate us to greater efforts in intercession. If trouble drives us to prayer and keeps us at it, then we will experience deliverance from trouble and the whole exercise will be very profitable! We cannot lose in the praying business."

"You make it all sound so cut and dried and easy," Ruth said with a sigh, "but I know deep down that you are right!" As she paused, the cloud of anxiety seemed to lift from her countenance and a smile broke across her face. "The Lord has just this minute reminded me of a verse in Psalm 50. 'Call

84

upon me in the day of trouble, I will deliver thee, and thou shalt glorify me.'"

"Yes!" Ron broke in excitedly, "and I just read recently that, 'if ye suffer for righteousness' sake, happy are ye; be not afraid of their terror, neither be troubled.'"[34]

"Oh, I wish I could remember exactly where that verse was," he said with exasperation.

Alan said slowly, "At least we can rejoice in this—if trouble is about to break over us for righteous intentions, then we need not fear. Is God not in total command? Will He not outwork any troubles for our greater benefit ultimately? We will certainly not seek to cause trouble, but if it comes for the cause and honor of God, then we can leave the issues in His hand."

A general ripple of approval came forth at this, and with a final brief word of prayer they separated to go their different ways, feeling somehow, in spite of some forebodings, that God was with them.

9

Everything but prayer

Bill was seated at his office desk when Alice Simpson, the office girl, peered around the edge of the door and said, "Mr. Frame is here to see you." For a minute Bill was a little confused, because James Frame had never visited him at the office in all the years they had been deacons in the church.

"Oh, er, show him in Alice," he mumbled, rapidly trying to compose himself while at the same time wondering what on earth James could want to see him about so urgently.

James Frame came into the office briskly, his gold, half-rimmed spectacles perched as ever firmly on the end of his nose. "Morning, Bill," he said in his brusque Civil Service manner. "Sorry if this is a bit of an intrusion, but I felt I just had to see you without delay "

"No, James, that's fine. I'm just going through samples of new materials. They're always bringing out something new in this space age technological era." Bill heard himself prattle out the words and was surprised at how banal they sounded. He was really stalling for time, trying to establish why James Frame should be in his office on a Thursday morning.

"Well, I won't waste your time. I'll come straight to the point," James rapped out, his voice betraying emotion not usually present. "We need to have an extraordinary business meeting at the church as soon as possible."

Bill struggled manfully to disguise his reaction, *"An extraordinary meeting!"* he exclaimed with his eyebrows raised questioningly. "Whatever for, James?"

"I thought you would have known why," James retorted, with a hint of rebuke in the tone of his voice.

"Really? I can't honestly say I can think of anything at the moment that would require the necessity of a special business meeting. Come to think of it, James, I can hardly remember us ever having one before."

"Even so," James snapped out, sweeping aside any possibility of discussion. "We certainly need one now!"

"OK!" Bill said, as dark thoughts and misgivings began to form inside his head. "Tell me, what's on your mind?"

"It's not just what's on my mind," James said, emphasizing the word *my* with a quick nod of the head. "Several of the members, and many of them of long and good standing, are objecting to the way Alan Kerr is trying to change things."

"And . . ." At this point James gave great emphasis to the word *and*. "And, he is not even the pastor! So we have decided to call a meeting to officially institute the proper calling of a pastor and ask Alan Kerr to stand down while we get different men to fill the vacancy meantime."

"We don't want any trouble," James added, affecting a self-righteous tone. "This is all for the good of the church and the happiness of its members."

Bill had been listening carefully to this oration when he broke in with a question. "Tell me first, James, who are these discontented members, and second, what is their complaint?"

"I could list them if necessary," James blustered somewhat. "And, as far as their complaint is concerned it is the same as mine."

88

"And what might that be?" Bill pressed further.

"Well," James usually prefaced his more momentous statements with a delayed *well*, "we object to a man who is almost a stranger to most of the people, trying to turn our church upside down and generally upsetting folks in the process."

"Nobody could disagree with that," Bill said, "but you'll have to be more specific, if you will."

"All this nonsense of his at the prayer meeting. Going on and on about a shopping list, and forcing people to get down on their knees and depriving us of information by cutting out the notices and . . ."

"Hey, wait a minute," Bill interjected. "I think we would have to examine the accuracy of these charges. For example, Alan has made me see that we have been wasting a lot of time on irrelevancies. He has also challenged me about the quality and biblical nature of my praying. And, to be fair, James," Bill said reprovingly, "I was present and can say that he certainly did not force anyone to get down on their knees. In fact I distinctly remember him saying that if anyone was unable to do so for good reason then it was all right."

"I might have known!" James Frame said disdainfully. "He's got you hooked on his radical ideas as well."

"No," Bill said deliberately, "it's just that I believe there is a lot of sense and biblical truth in what he's been saying and I don't think that you or anyone else have any concrete complaints that you can bring against him."

"We'll see about that," James flared up angrily. "After all these years we are not going to stand for our church being wrested from us by some fanatical radical of unknown pedigree."

Bill couldn't resist asking demurely, "And does Jean agree with these views of yours?"

He had been thinking, "The voice is Jacob's voice, but the hands are the hands of Esau."[35] Bill knew that Jean exerted undue influence on James and he had heard much of her voice in James's assertions.

"Of course she does, and so do many others also!" James huffed.

Perhaps it was not the most opportune moment for Ron to arrive on the scene, but as Bill reflected later, "the Lord is sovereign in every aspect of Providence."[36]

Alice had mentioned to Ron when he entered Bill's office that Mr. Frame was with him. Ron nodded, then poked his head around the door as usual. Bill and Ron had a special relationship beyond that of boss and employee, principally as a result of Bill's early influence in bringing Ron to Earlton Baptist Church where he was subsequently saved.

"Excuse me, Bill," Ron said lightheartedly. Then seeing James Frame, he quipped sarcastically, "Hi, James. Don't see you here very often."

Bill was just about to ask what he wanted when James Frame, still somewhat heated at Bill's apparent support for Alan Kerr, blurted out, "You'll soon know the reason why I'm here and so will the rest of the church."

As Ron paused, his head still peeking round the half open door, Bill rose to bar his entry. James Frame was very wound up by now, however, and young Ron, not particularly discerning, refused to back off from the situation.

Sensing that he was about to hear some revelation that would enliven the drudgery of the daily round, Ron then burst into the room and, looking James in the eye, said, "What do you mean, James?"

Bill knew that it was a lost cause at this point. He slumped back resignedly into his chair, awaiting the outcome.

The office door had barely closed behind Ron when

James went on the offensive. "I've been in this church for over 25 years and I'm not going to stand by and see it destroyed by virtual strangers." He then covered the same ground with Ron that he had gone over with Bill. "But how can you understand this, Ron? You're too young to know about these things." He almost hissed the words, his beady eyes now glaring angrily over the half spectacles.

Ron, with all the tact and diplomacy of callow youth, replied, "I certainly don't know what you are on about!"

James Frame was fuming in frustration now and fueling his anger and frustration was a sneaking suspicion that this young upstart was not at all swayed by his arguments.

"I think that Alan is the best thing that has happened to this church since I joined, and I certainly hope that he will be made pastor before long," Ron said defiantly.

James could take no more of this. Enraged, he rose in such haste that he knocked over his chair. "I'll be going then," he said, his voice rising in an angry crescendo. "But don't think this is the end of the matter, and you can inform any others who entertain the same foolish notions as you do that it is not. Good morning!"

Alice was startled by the office door banging and the hurried departure of James Frame as he stomped out.

Ron was a bit stunned. "What on earth is all that about?" he asked in bewilderment.

"That is the prelude to a nasty storm that is about to break over the church and cause a lot of damage and heartbreak," Bill said as he leaned back in his chair and looked at the ceiling in a weary, detached kind of a way.

Ron left the office agitated and confused. Although it was the lunch hour, he wasn't exactly feeling hungry. Almost unconsciously he found himself heading for the Christian book shop with its air of tranquillity and timelessness. Mrs. Shearer was busy behind the counter arranging books on the shelves.

"Oh, it's nice to see you, Ron," she said, her face crinkling into a sunny smile. "I'm just about to put the kettle on. Why not have a cup of tea with us?"

"Martha, eh, Miss Wood," she corrected herself quickly, "will be here in a minute to join us."

Ron soon unfolded the events of the morning to the two old ladies. He was somewhat disconcerted by the apparent calm and lack of excitement by which they received his report. They were such good listeners, too. "A rare commodity," he thought, "even among Christian people at times."

"It's true," Martha said softly, "that Brother Alan has been quite blunt, and some might even say unfeeling. But there is a great need of reformation in the church, and I'm sure that the enemy is not going to allow this without his opposition."

Mrs. Shearer had been listening attentively and now she spoke quietly. "Andrew Bonar, the old Scots divine, once said,

> As the king of Syria commanded his servants to fight with neither great nor small, but only with the King of Israel, so the Prince of the power of the air seems to bend all the force of his attack against the spirit of prayer. If he should prove victorious there, he has won the day."

Martha nodded wisely at this interjection and then remarked, "Brother Alan has no doubt raised some hackles with his plain speaking. But is there *never* a time for strong exhortation? Was this not how the prophets of old addressed situations of indolence and neglect? I do believe that the church has suffered from a surfeit of nice, inoffensive homilies and an almost total absence of exhortative preaching from what I can gather."

"More power to Alan," she said elatedly. "I cannot believe that the Lord has watched over this church for almost 90 years just to let it subside in prayerlessness and declension. Mr. Hudson Taylor, founder of the China Inland Mission, once quoted Newton when he said:

> He cannot have taught us to trust in His Name,
> And thus far have brought us to put us to shame."

She finished with an emphatic nod of her head.

Ron was quite mesmerized by all of this for he could not recall these gentle ladies ever before getting so excited about anything. Especially, he thought, when they were so calm and collected at the outset.

Mrs. Shearer rose up at this juncture to clear away the dishes from the table, saying as she did so, "I only pray that James Frame and his friends have as much concern for the church and its growth in grace as Brother Alan does."

"Seems I'm learning something profitable from this situation, too," Ron said somewhat ruefully. "If Alan has got a little carried away in his zeal and emphasis, I know for sure that I got carried away a bit by these books by Bounds. They certainly fired me up. Maybe I should have been more selective about who I spoke to regarding them and less pressurizing with my opinions."

"Now don't you fret about it, Ron," Mrs. Shearer said confidently and kindly. "None of us would come to great harm if we followed the example of Mr. Bounds. As for Alan, he's a good man and only benefit can come of his reminding us and challenging us to make our praying more biblical. When you think about it, as I recall, he only emphasized three sound principles. I wrote them down as he spoke, so let me just read them to you again."

She read from her list:

1. The need to pray with a proper motive—James 4:3
2. The need of unanimity in our praying—Matthew 18:19
3. The necessity of faith in our asking—James 5:14,15

"I believe," Mrs. Shearer continued, "that's the gist of what Alan has brought to our attention so far. Well, I know it is unless my notes have changed themselves."

She laughed at this, just as Ron interrupted to say, "No, they certainly did not, because I noted these points myself at the meeting and that's exactly what he said."

"Regarding the methodology and format of the gatherings," Miss Wood said, "I do believe that Satan has managed to successfully whittle away the time we actually spend in prayer and replace it with needless verbosity. Anything, everything, but prayer itself. That's his strategy. So I have personally been much encouraged by Brother Alan's courage in addressing our bad habits and traditions."

At this point, Ron looked at his watch and leapt to his feet, amazed to find that he was already late for work. "Hey!" he exclaimed suddenly, "I've got to be off. Thanks for the tea and especially for the fellowship. You've both been a great help and blessing to me today." He left the book shop in a completely different frame of mind than when he arrived. In fact, despite being late for work, he found himself singing several favorite hymns as he hurried to the workshop.

"He is a fine young man," Martha said to Mrs. Shearer after Ron had gone.

"Yes, he is, and I believe that the Lord has His hand upon him for some future work," Mrs. Shearer replied. "It's so encouraging to see young men genuinely interested in the things of God these days. Let's take a moment to commend all these things to the Lord."

"Dear Lord," Martha began, "please receive our grateful thanks that all things are in Thy precious hands. Do bless Alan and grant him great wisdom and keep your hand upon young Ron in his youthful zeal."

"Help James Frame," Mrs. Shearer added. "Guide him aright and restrain him from anything that would encourage revenge in his soul or in the souls of others. Amen."

10

The prayer meeting is for the glory of God

It was just before the start of the prayer meeting that James Frame accosted Alan on his way to the vestry.

"Do you think that I and several of the members could have a word with you?"

"I don't think that just prior to the prayer meeting is the best time, James, but I would be happy to meet with you at the end of the service."

James was not too happy about this.

"Well, I suppose that will have to do then," he reluctantly agreed, sensing Alan's reticence.

The group of which he was spokesman had planned to meet with Alan and Bill before the meeting and then leave the building. Alan's insistence on gathering after the prayer meeting had at least forced them to be present, although this was not his primary reason for so acting.

Knowing that the hostile group comprised of the Frames, the Drurys, the Wilsons, and several others who had been enlisted, Alan determined meanwhile to proceed as normal and to concentrate on the ministry previously embarked upon. He knew that anything he said would be minutely examined to see if it could be construed in any way as "getting at" the opposition.

In the prayer meeting, Alan said slowly in measured tones, "We have considered the necessity of proper motive, the need of unanimity, and the requirement of faith in our requests if we are to receive answers from heaven. Let us remind ourselves again that true prayer has certain laws, conditions, and limits which must he observed. We cannot merely articulate the first thing that comes into our heads in an undisciplined, impulsive manner. We remind you that the Apostle James has made it clear[37] that we can ask aright or ask amiss." A quick glance toward the back row confirmed that the rebels were suffering in sullen silence, waiting to pounce on anything they thought could remotely be seen as referring to them personally.

Alan continued, "We are not to think that prayer can be utilized to coerce God to bend to our demands. Rather we must be concerned that our requests have a degree of harmony with the mind of God. We must establish also, insofar as we can, that what we ask is not against the will of God in any given circumstance."

Alan began to draw to a close by saying, "Perhaps one great fallacy that exists among many Christian people and has been propagated by certain sections of the church, is this distortion of truth. I refer to the Scripture in John 14:14, 'If ye shall ask anything in my name, I will do it.' This has unfortunately produced a brandishing of the name of Jesus and a repetition of the name as if the very vocalizing of it, especially in emotional outbursts, had a magical power detached from any pre-conditions. It is error to seek to use the sacred name as some kind of totem, and to think that by repeated insertion of it into our asking, we can call down answers from heaven. This gets close to the performance of the prophets of

Baal and their antics on Mount Carmel.[38] This is not what is meant by asking in the name of Jesus."

"To pray in the name of Jesus involves praying for that which we believe the Lord Jesus Christ can identify with or approve of. The mere insertion of the phrase, *for Jesus sake,* or *in Jesus' name* can often be nothing more or less than vain repetition. There is another fallacy, popular today, that we can *claim it.* This is also reprehensible. This deception proceeds from a defective view of the sovereignty of God. What can the First Cause of all things possibly owe to such miserable creatures as we? Surely we deserve nothing from Him, and indeed the vessel praying properly recognizes this and prays accordingly. This presumptuous attitude actually constitutes praying in our own name and will not gain the desired response from God."

A good number of the congregation, perhaps around thirty folks, listened with rapt attention to Alan's exhortation. James Frame and his retinue were unmistakably uneasy. They shuffled nervously and looked undecided as to what to do next.

"Let's turn to the Lord now and concentrate on these items," Alan said. "Remember how we have considered the inadvisability, if not impossibility, of being genuinely burdened for many matters at one time. We will limit our praying to those things we definitely know that each of us here is conversant with and unitedly concerned about. We can actually hinder weaker brethren in matters of prayer if we insist in overloading them with a surfeit of items or persons with which they are totally unfamiliar. If you feel strongly about areas that are not of universal interest to us as a church, then pray about them at home.[39]"

"First, then, let's petition the Lord about souls being saved and added to the church."

Albert Higgins, perhaps through faulty hearing or lack of understanding or maybe even lack of attention, was first into the fray. "Lord!" he boomed in a loud voice, "you know that our last pastor, Andrew Paterson, was a good man. Bless his ministry in his new church and let him know that we miss him here."

Alan grimaced as his face pressed into the back of the chair. He was relieved that no one could see his expression as he wondered what he had to do to get people to understand. Albert was old and probably hadn't been listening, but it was just typical of the kind of behavior that Alan was striving to correct.

Albert rambled on without too much to say, but this was no deterrent to the length of time he managed to occupy. On each occasion when it seemed he had reached a conclusion, a new germ of thought spawned more irrelevant rambling.

Alan noticed how people got fidgety at this performance, and though Albert was a little senile, Satan was still able to utilize the rambling to kill the prayer meeting before it got started.

Ron tried to rescue the situation and did pray with some spirit and direction, adhering to the subject requested, but to little avail.

One bright and encouraging interlude was Jack Kemp's first faltering steps in prayer. Briefly, but sincerely, he prayed, "Lord save some souls just as you have saved me, and give me the opportunity to witness in my workplace with the hope of getting some of my workmates to come to the Gospel service."

* * *

"I'm afraid that there aren't seats for everyone," Alan

100

said to James Frame and the group who assembled in the vestry at the close of the service.

"That's no problem," James Frame said coldly. "We don't intend to be here very long anyway."

"Well, what is it you want to see me about?" Alan asked pleasantly, looking over his shoulder at Bill Morgan whom he had asked to be present at the meeting.

He could sense that Bill was uncomfortable, but he knew that the time had come for him to take his stand, too, and that the experience would be good for him.

"We won't beat about the bush," James said curtly. "I and several of the members of the church, some of whom are present, are unhappy with the way things have been going since our pastor, Andrew Paterson, left. We feel that there is a disruptive influence in the church and that you are responsible for this."

James was cut off at this point by the intervention of Monica Drury's strident tones.

"Yes," she said excitedly, "and you're not even the pastor either! You should remember this before you go about tampering with the services and forcing your ideas and regulations on us."

She would have gone on in an increasing crescendo, but her husband interrupted to say, "She feels very strongly about this, and so do we!" He looked at the others as he said this and a few incoherent grunts and assorted mumblings apparently confirmed this.

Alan hadn't said anything at this juncture, preferring to hear what they had to say so he might assess his response to the accusations and disaffections with his ministry.

"Friends," he began in conciliatory fashion, "I would like to remind you that I never applied for the post of pastor, and indeed only agreed to take it on a temporary basis until

101

the Lord should bring His man for the job."

"Yes, be that as it may," Roger Drury said roughly, "but it does look to us like you are trying to take over and change everything, especially at the prayer meeting."

Alan looked Roger straight in the eye and said in a low modulated tone of voice, "Very well then, Roger, perhaps you or one of the others might tell me how the prayer meeting ought to be conducted."

"I don't profess to be an expert," Roger said gruffly, "but I didn't see anything wrong with the way we've had the meetings for years now."

Jean Frame cut in at this point in the sickly sweet, affected voice she reserved for occasions when she was trying to sound spiritual. "Of course none of us is an expert at praying, but the Lord has heard all our prayers in the past. He has helped us when we were raising money for the new organ and even blessed the young people when we prayed for their sponsored walks and marathon Bible reading events." She sniffed audibly at this point, as if it were a prelude to the shedding of a few crystal tears.

"But *what* is the aim of the prayer meeting?" Alan pressed with insistence.

Phil Wilson coughed nervously and said, "Well, I think it is to try and keep us together and to ask God to help us maintain the Baptist witness that has been in this town for nearly a hundred years."

"Yes! And not split it up and try to force things on people that they don't want! That's not how to preserve unity!" Roger interjected strongly, looking around for approval.

Gwen Wilson whispered something in her husband's ear and he asked that they might be excused as his wife was feeling ill. They slipped out, to Alan's relief, though he did notice that Gwen's face looked very pallid and drawn.

"With all due respect, friends, I don't think that any of you have given a satisfactory answer to my question," Alan said. "I consider it a very important question, the answer to which might help us resolve our present difficulties."

"I don't see the relevance of it," James Frame said disdainfully.

"Just bear with me while I lay a few things before you, and I'll be brief so you can all go home and think about them before coming to any hasty conclusions," Alan said.

He then opened his Bible. "Throughout the Word of God, especially in the Book of Psalms and all through the New Testament, we are commanded as our chief end to glorify God. I remember as a child I went to a Presbyterian church Sunday school and the first question in the catechism was, 'What is the chief and highest end of man?' The answer was, 'Man's chief end is to glorify God and enjoy Him forever.'[40] We Baptists certainly have no quarrel with that particular statement."[41] [42]

Alan continued, "Now, you'll notice that nowhere is it suggested that the prayer meeting, or any other church meeting for that matter, is to be convened to please man. The prayer meeting then, primarily, is to glorify God. To pray for souls? Yes! To seek God for help in our witness and the extension of the Kingdom of God? Yes! To pray earnestly for one another? Yes! But far above any of these things, to glorify God! So we must begin to deal with any outstanding things that would oppose such a high and noble purpose. For that reason I must disagree with the answers you have given to my question tonight."

"We don't need a sermon," James Frame said icily. "We just came here to tell you that we don't want you continuing to lead our services."

"If you would just listen briefly and consider, you would

see that I am simply defending biblical principles. How we glorify God is not left to our imaginations," Alan continued a little wearily. "We have a letter handed down from heaven to earth, the Bible, which clearly sets out three fundamental propositions. First, we are told how we may glorify God and enjoy Him forever. Second, we see that the Word of God is set forth in Old and New Testaments. And, third, we understand that God's rule is the only one by which we must go."

Alan knew this was elementary, but nevertheless it was certain from the discussion that the group had no clear understanding of such basics. It was obvious that they did not even have an idea of the purposes behind a prayer meeting. How long had these people sought to serve God without a reference to the Holy Spirit? So long without the manifest presence of the Holy Spirit in their gatherings, could they even recognize His absence? Did these people realize that the Scriptures had instructions regarding prayer and its essential ingredients?[43] [44] [45] [46] [47]

Alan's train of thought was broken by the group getting to their feet and preparing to leave. As they did so, Roger Drury blustered irritably, "We can all interpret the Bible to suit our own opinions, if we like!"

"That is possibly the truest statement you've made tonight, my friend," Alan quietly thought as he joined the exodus. He knew they were leaving to plot their next move and this was only the first salvo in what could become a bitter and messy conflict.

As he bade them goodnight, Alan found himself thinking, "Truly, man by nature does not have the glory of God as his central compelling ambition."

* * *

104

"Is that you, Alan?" Carol called out as he came through the front outside door.

"Yes, Carol. Are the kids in bed now?"

"When I saw that you were going to be late, I had our devotional time with them myself."

"Oh, yes. Good," Alan said a little absentmindedly. "Carol," he exclaimed suddenly, "do you ever wish that we were back in India?"

11

Trouble focuses our minds

Mrs. Shearer and Miss Wood had just finished their morning devotions when Bill Morgan came through the front door of the shop.

"Oh, Bill, how nice to see you," Mrs. Shearer said with a welcoming smile. "Didn't expect to see you here at this time of the morning."

Martha lived very close to the shop and she came every morning when they usually opened around 9 a.m. The first thing Mrs. Shearer and Martha did after breakfast each morning was to have a time of prayer together. There were seldom any customers before ten.

Bill looked a bit troubled, as though he had not had a good night's sleep.

"Just putting the kettle on, Bill," Martha called from the little kitchen at the back of the shop.

"Er, not for me," Bill stammered. Then quickly correcting himself he said, "Thanks, Martha, on second thought, I think I will."

"We don't get many customers at this time of the morning," Mrs. Shearer said cheerily as she led Bill to the little back room. Bill seated himself on an old armchair and was quite relieved to sink down on to its creaking springs.

"Is anything wrong, Bill?" Mrs. Shearer asked quietly.

* * *

"Do you want me to come with you?" Phil Wilson anxiously asked his wife Gwen.

"No, there's no need for you to take a morning off work. I'll be fine. But you know, Phil, I must admit I was surprised that the doctor arranged for me to go so soon for tests at the hospital."

"Look, Gwen," Phil began, "I can easily take the morning off and go with you for the results of these tests. After all, I'm just as anxious as you are to hear what the doctor has to say. You have been losing weight for months now."

Gwen would have liked Phil to accompany her, but she knew that he had several important projects to attend to at his office. Therefore she found herself saying, "No, I'll be all right, Phil. I'll give you all the information when you get home from work in the evening."

* * *

Gwen gripped the arms of the chair till her knuckles turned white. Her lips were clamped tightly together. She felt the room revolve and she almost fainted. Behind the desk the doctor spoke the words as sympathetically as he could, but he could not lessen their fearful import.

"Terminal?" she gasped, her face ashen and the words barely audible.

"Let me get my secretary to phone your husband. Tell me how we may contact him and we'll arrange for him to come and take you home."

108

Mrs. Shearer's question galvanized Bill into response. "Yes, I'm afraid there is something wrong, seriously wrong." He reminded them of the events of Wednesday evening, finding it hard to believe that it actually happened. He was a little taken aback that the unfolding of events had not produced a more profound effect on the old sisters, but he put this down to the fact that they had not been in the church long. He also realized that nothing ever seemed to upset their equilibrium.

Martha, rummaging among the boxes of books she was unpacking and putting on the book shelves, nodded sagaciously as she spoke. "It's the warfare. We need not be surprised. 'In the world ye shall have tribulation: but be of good cheer, I have overcome the world.'[48] Now we need to understand that stern conflict makes the experienced warrior. Only battles produce conquerors. Our pilgrim way is one of warfare because we walk through an opposing world. It is a way of victory if we walk therein with Jesus. So much depends upon the soul's position in faith. If from the midst of worldly associations it views Jesus afar off, it will be often overcome. But if it views the world and its associations from a walk of close fellowship with Him, it will always conquer for it is ever the place of victory."

Bill looked across to Martha and saw that she was reading from an old book. She caught his glance and said, "This old book[49] has been a treasure to me for over 60 years now. It was given to me by my father when I was a girl."

Bill rose to go and Mrs. Shearer said, "Bill, we must pray for Alan. He has set foot on enemy territory and there is going to be a storm. Still, we need to remember that the Lord uses the storm to bring us to Himself. Circumstances that empty a man of self, prepare him for fuller revelations of God. How great was the wind that blew before the Lord rebuked it, that the disciples might better understand their great need and the great love that overshadowed them. The whole church, not just Alan, is going to feel the storm."[50]

So deep had been the impression the old sisters had made upon him, that Bill was certain that he would not be able to concentrate on his business matters when he arrived back at the office.

After Bill left, Martha and Mrs. Shearer were putting more of the books on the shelves and discussing the latest events.

"When we first gave that book on prayer to young Ron, I had no idea that it would soon become a contentious issue in the church."

"No, my dear," Martha replied, "and we weren't even members of Earlton Baptist Church at that time either."

"True, Martha, and Andrew Paterson was pastor then. My, my, how quickly things have changed over these past few months."

At this point the two ladies were interrupted by the phone ringing.

Mrs. Shearer said, "I'll answer it, dear," and she lifted the receiver.

Martha could sense by the tone of Mrs. Shearer's voice and the anxious look on her face that something serious had happened.

"I'll be right over," she said. "I'll leave Martha to look after the shop."

Martha waited patiently, inquisitively.

Mrs. Shearer said gravely, "It's Gwen Wilson. That was her husband Phil. I'm afraid it's very bad news. She has cancer."

"Cancer?" Martha said incredulously. "But I never even knew she was ill."

"Yes, I did know that she hasn't been well," Mrs. Shearer said, "but I never dreamt that it was anything like this. They've only given her a few months to live at best."

She put on her old dark coat and hat, and, being reassured that Martha would look after the shop till she returned, she set out for the Wilson's home on the outskirts of the town. Martha picked up her Bible and opening it to Isaiah 61, read, "To comfort all that mourn." She prayed that her friend might be enabled to do this.

* * *

It was around lunch time when Bill finally arrived at the workplace. The dark gloomy day with intermittent drizzle of rain matched his gloomy mood. As he entered the front door he almost bumped into Ron and Jack Kemp. Jack had called to see if Ron would go to lunch with him at the local cafe.

"You boys off to lunch?" Bill said with a cheerfulness he didn't exactly feel inside.

"Yes!" Ron responded. "Why don't you join us?"

Bill paused for a moment before replying. "Yes, why not. Look, you two hang on a moment and let me check that there's nothing urgently demanding my attention and I'll be right with you."

Bill was actually needing some fellowship to lighten the burden he was feeling over the church situation.

"At least that's one bright ray of encouragement," he thought. "Young Jack has made great advances since he trusted the Lord." His steps quickened and even the burden seemed more bearable in the light of Jack's progress in the things of God. Bill suddenly found himself singing quietly under his

111

breath as he went into his office:

> He giveth more grace when the burdens grow greater;
> He sendeth more strength when the labors increase.
> To added afflictions He addeth His mercy;
> To multiplied trials, His multiplied peace.

He got quite carried away at this and began to sing the chorus of the hymn with increasing volume and enjoyment, heedless of whether anyone was listening or not!

> His love has no limit;
> His grace has no measure;
> His pow'r has no boundary known unto men;
> For out of His infinite riches in Jesus,
> He giveth, and giveth, and giveth again!

By this time Bill was quite rejuvenated by the uplifting theme of the hymn[51] and his flagging spirit somewhat revived.

Seated round the table in the cafe, the two young zealots wasted no time in directing the conversation into spiritual channels. Bill could not help noticing this and it brought a lump to his throat, which he hastily concealed. To see their interest in Christ and their desire to serve Him was quite moving.

"Did you finish reading that book by Bounds yet?" Ron exclaimed.

"No, but I'm fairly well through it now and it's certainly challenging me," Bill said. "But you know, Ron, there are other good books in the world, too! Mr. Bounds isn't the only man who has ever written books on prayer."

"I know, I know that," Ron said with mild exasperation. "But I believe that the Lord put that book into my hand at just the right time and meant me to read it for some specific reason. Jack's been reading the other one[52] that Mrs. Shearer

112

gave me, and he loves it. Don't you, Jack?"

Jack replied affirmatively, then he continued very respectfully, "Maybe you could help me, Bill?"

"Oh no!" Bill thought. "I can't keep up with these two young firebrands. Still, I must try and encourage them." So, he asked cheerfully, "What's on your mind, Jack?"

"Well," Jack said seriously, "if prayer is as important as this book makes out, and the Bible seems to back this up according to what Alan has been preaching, why is it that so few members come to the prayer meetings?"

"These young converts know how to ask the most embarrassing questions," Bill said to himself with a sigh and a wry smile.

"Jack," Bill said, looking him straight in the eye, "that's a good question! Now Ron here knows that we've discussed similar matters in the past few weeks, and I have had to confess ignorance about many of them. Alan is the man to ask for a comprehensive answer to this. However, I'll give you my opinion, for what it's worth.

"I believe there are two main reasons for this situation," he continued. "First, people have not been properly taught and sufficiently exhorted about prayer. Second, the prayer meeting is deadly boring for most people, and those who have the responsibility for leading it seem afraid to face up to this reality. I believe that if you were to ask the folks in most churches about their prayer meeting, and you pressed them for a totally honest answer, they would say the same."

Jack seemed slightly stunned by this forthright declaration, but not Ron.

"I'm really glad to hear you saying this because I believe that it's absolutely true. Before Alan started to try and correct things, we were dying by degrees. It was like the old fairy story line, 'The King has got no clothes on.' Everybody knew it, but nobody had the courage to say so," Ron said.

"Well," Bill responded, "I'm not sure that everybody knew things were not what they ought to be, specifically if we concede that many haven't been properly instructed, and years of familiarity with deadness has cauterized them. However, we know from experience that whenever someone tries to tackle the status quo, or traditional practices, they have a tough job on their hands. The best way we can help Alan and the church in this problem is for us to apply ourselves to pray for God's intervention in the situation."

* * *

Phil and Gwen Wilson lived in an apartment in a blonde stone traditional terrace, quite near to the church in the suburbs of the town. Mrs. Shearer caught a bus almost immediately and arrived at the Wilson's home about half an hour after receiving the phone call. There was a security door entry system and she pushed the button opposite the Wilson's name.

Phil Wilson answered instantly. "Please come up, Mrs. Shearer. We're on the first floor." He paused, sounding embarrassed, then quickly added, "What am I thinking about, you've been here several times before."

The Wilsons had often gone into the book shop, even long before Mrs. Shearer had begun attending Earlton Baptist Church. Although Mrs. Shearer was of a much deeper spiritual caliber than the Wilsons, she always had a friendly relationship with them and it was not the first time she had visited their home. She went straight to the bedroom and found Gwen, ashen faced and drawn, propped up in bed with pillows surrounding her. Gwen had been crying and her eyes were red rimmed. Phil hovered pale and nervous as he stood by the bay window which overlooked the busy street.

"How are you, Gwen, my dear," Mrs. Shearer asked, as she sat by the bedside after hugging Gwen.

She held her hand as she continued to speak in a quiet voice, "Let's read a few verses of Scripture."

The Wilsons were strangely encouraged by Mrs. Shearer's presence as she seemed to emanate something of the nearness of the Lord, so humble and gracious was her spirit.

After reading Psalm 112 and emphasizing the seventh verse, Mrs. Shearer prayed and committed the whole matter into God's hands. When she finished she turned to Phil and asked, "Have you told Alan yet?"

There was an awkward silence and then Gwen began to sob aloud, saying, "We went to that meeting and told him that we wanted him out of the pulpit."

She was overcome and could not continue. Her husband came over and put his arms around her, saying, "We didn't understand, dear. James just talked us into it. We were confused." He tailed off into silence, not knowing what to say.

Mrs. Shearer spoke softly, but with that aura of authority she seemed to possess in spiritual issues, "Now don't you give it a second thought. Alan is a good man. He would never hold that against you even if you had wanted to get rid of him, which I know you really didn't. I remember in India when my husband died, Alan was a great comfort to me. He and Carol had just arrived as young missionaries on the field and I hardly knew them, but they were so kind and helpful. I really don't know what I would have done without them. I'll just go and phone him now, if I may."

They both nodded, feeling a heavy weight of guilt that they should have been party to any move to oppose Alan.

"Strange, too," Phil thought, "that we're not sending for

James Frame or any of the agitators at this time of need. Trouble surely focuses the mind and sharpens perspectives."

Alan was shocked and stunned when Mrs. Shearer told him of the tragedy that had overtaken the Wilsons. "If it's not too late, or inconvenient, I'll come over right away."

Mrs. Shearer confirmed that it would be all right and that she would be there when he arrived.

12

The Lord chastens those whom He loves

As Alan drove to the Wilson's house in the drizzly and dreary November cold, his mind flashed back to a similar situation fifteen years earlier.

At that time he and Carol were commencing their missionary activity in India. They had recently moved to the city of Hyderabad and they were just beginning to learn their way around the twin cities of Hyderabad and Secunderabad. Secunderabad had been a cantonment area for British troops during the period of British rule, and considerable evidence of this still remained long after the departure of the troops in the forties.

Peter Shearer and his wife Margaret, who had been missionaries in India since 1939, were about to retire when the Kerrs arrived.

On that October evening 15 years prior Alan was startled by the shrill ring of the telephone in the old mission house in Secunderabad. Margaret Shearer's calm voice—*the same calm voice that had just summoned him to the Wilson's home*—made a similar request.

"Alan, can you come over quickly? It's Peter. I think

he's had a heart attack. It looks serious," Mrs. Shearer had said.

Leaving Carol with the children, Alan soon found himself alone on a dusty street searching in all directions for an auto. The auto was the favored means of taxi for the vast majority of the people who could afford such luxury. In reality it was a motorized tricycle, usually painted bright yellow and able to officially seat three behind the driver. Autos were driven recklessly and with wild abandon, weaving in erratic suicidal lunges between masses of pedestrians, cyclists, trucks, and handcarts. Auto drivers seemed bent on violating the few traffic regulations that existed.

Alan finally hailed an auto and quickly gave the driver instructions. He prayed as he rode wildly and dangerously to his destination. For once his mind was totally detached from the mad swerving of the auto and the incessant blasting of horns on every conceivable form of vehicle.

Alan hadn't known the Shearers for more than six months, but in that short time he had come to the conclusion that Peter Shearer was a choice, holy servant of God who manifested quality spiritual dedication.

The first time Alan met Peter was at a prayer meeting in the prayer house on the edge of the city. The prayer house had a thatched roof with brick pillars supporting it and a dirt floor. Otherwise it was open without any windows or doors. During prayer meetings the sisters sat on one side and the brethren on the other.

Peter had a mane of white hair and was dressed in plain white shirt and trousers. He carried a large Telegu language Bible from which he was bringing an exhortation on prayer. Alan was not at that time very fluent in Telegu, but he did catch the gist of the message which remained with him ever since. Peter's words carried force and power because he did

118

not merely *have* a message, Peter Shearer *was* the message!

He had begun to speak in quiet, resonant tones from a portion of Micah 7:7, "I have been almost thirty years in South India now. During that time I have been enabled by God through the agency of the Holy Spirit to continue regularly and steadfastly in prayer. Part of my motivation has been my confidence that the Lord does hear and answer prayer. I have also learned the hard lesson of being able on many occasions to receive a 'no' from God."

Alan could virtually see and hear him again. There he stood, illuminated by a single paraffin lamp with the eager faces of the dark-skinned congregation reflecting their love and respect for this man.

"My God will hear me," Peter emphasized. "And our confidence tonight is that we are in the presence of the living God who heard us yesterday and will hear us again, for He changes not. Is He not the same God? Has He not been faithful? Is He the God of all truth? Establish the answers to these questions in your hearts, dear friends, and your faith will rise. What enemy shall triumph over us! Look around you tonight, brethren, your very attendance here once again is encouraging evidence that you believe with the prophet of old that, 'My God will hear me!' Now let us strive again to imbibe three basic principles for acceptable public intercession."

Peter looked at the intent faces and then asked, "Who can remember the three basic rules?"

A number of eager hands shot up and the paraffin lamp reflected numerous stalagmites of shadow pointing up from the earthen floor. Peter selected one of the young men, "Yes, Daniel?"

"Fervency,[53] accuracy,[54] brevity.[55]"

"Excellent!" Peter beamed. "Let's now concentrate on these unconverted souls who have been coming into the Gospel meetings. Then, let us pray for the plot of land next door so that we might acquire it to enable us to extend the prayer house. We can finish with brief relevant requests that God lays upon your hearts."

Alan was impressed by the clear, orderly, precise instructions that confined praying to specific matters, not so many matters as to confuse or dissipate the unity of purpose of the praying. Yet, Peter's instructions left ample opportunity for the Holy Spirit to impress the hearer's minds with relevant issues.

* * *

It was only as the traffic lights changed suddenly to red that Alan came back to earth with a jolt. It took him a moment to realize that he was not back in India with Peter Shearer in the prayer hall, but instead was only a mile or so from the Wilsons home on a distressing visitation. He quickly found a parking place near the entrance to the Wilson's flat and was soon at the front door.

Phil Wilson was a little bit flustered and embarrassed as he opened the apartment door to Alan. Mrs. Shearer came over quickly to join them.

"Good to see you, Alan. Come right in. You've met Phil and Gwen."

Alan greeted them and soon made the Wilsons feel relaxed as he shrugged off their apologies regarding their participation in recent events.

"We shouldn't have been at that meeting," Gwen said tearfully, "but James Frame talked us into it."

Alan interjected at this point, "Listen, you have enough to think about without going over all of that. The Lord knows none of us has all the answers in these kinds of situations.

120

Let's just forget about it."

Alan was surprised at how ashen faced and sickly Gwen looked since he had last seen her. She was obviously very ill, and though he tried not to think so, she looked like she had not long to live.

"Maybe this would not have come upon us if we had not decided to go along with James Frame and the others in opposing what God was doing in the church," she sobbed quietly.

Mrs. Shearer looked out of the corner of her eye at Alan as Gwen said this. She gave the impression that she had an answer to this lament, but she was refraining from any comment.

Alan sat at the bedside and said in quiet but firm tones, "Now, Gwen, God is not in the business of punishing His children in vindictive ways under any circumstances, even if we do err at times. Christian people are not exempt from sicknesses any more than they are exempt from other afflictions. The Lord chastens those whom He loves.[56] It is not necessarily a mark of God's displeasure when we become sick. Remember how Mary and Martha could say to the Savior, 'He whom thou lovest is sick.'[57]

"Notice," Alan said quite intensely, "It wasn't, 'He whom thou hatest is sick.' Nevertheless, it is quite usual when we are ill to question God's love toward us more than at other times. Don't fret over such things."

Mrs. Shearer nodded wisely in agreement with the sentiments Alan was expressing.

At this point, he gently took hold of Gwen's hand and consoled her by saying, "Sickness is not automatically a manifestation of God's disfavor toward His children. This is a mistake that Job's friends made, and sadly many Christians of certain persuasions make today."

121

Alan concluded the time with prayer and offered to give Mrs. Shearer a lift home. After a period of silence in the car, she broke the quietness by saying, "You know, Alan, it's a great pity that so often it takes severe afflictions to produce a better heart within us."

Alan could only murmur in agreement and be grateful that even in the tragedy which the Wilsons were experiencing, there were still amazingly good ingredients woven through the sadness and grief.[58]

"You know, sister," Alan said just before they arrived outside Mrs. Shearer's front door, "it's easy to believe in the sovereignty of God until such an illness as Gwen has comes upon us."

"Well, Alan, I'm sure that the Wilsons really appreciated your visit with them. You can be assured that Martha and I will be praying much about the situation. We will be asking the Lord to give you much wisdom in the various matters which are pressing in upon you at this time. Thank you very much for the lift home. We'll see you soon."

13

God can bring good out of apparent disaster

Martha Wood and Mrs. Shearer had just finished their morning devotions in the little back room of the book shop.

"I'm glad that we were able to bring our concern about Gwen Wilson's condition before the Lord this morning," Mrs. Shearer said softly to Martha.

"Yes indeed, and I think it was also timely that we asked the Lord expressly to give Alan wisdom in the situation," Martha replied.

Pausing for a moment's reflection, she continued, "You know, Margaret, I also have great peace concerning our fervent prayers that God would appoint Alan as pastor before very long."

Mrs. Shearer nodded in agreement.

"By the way, I phoned Phil and told him I would be coming over to visit Gwen after lunch," Martha said to Mrs. Shearer, as they sat and had a cup of tea before going into the shop for the day's work.

"Are you sure that you are up to going over there, dear?" Mrs. Shearer kindly asked Martha.

"Of course I am," Martha replied somewhat indignantly.

"I may be eighty years old, but I'm not helpless yet!"

"Well, then, you must be careful getting on and off the bus," Mrs. Shearer said, inwardly admiring the spirit that Martha displayed, which greatly belied her age.

* * *

It was around two o'clock when Martha sat down at Gwen's bedside.

"Mrs. Shearer and I have been much in prayer about your whole situation, Gwen. We have also sought the Lord that he would make Himself near to you in this time of affliction and trial. I know that you will also be encouraged that the church will be definitely praying for you tomorrow night at the prayer meeting."

They talked back and forth awhile before they were interrupted by the doorbell ringing. Phil went to answer it and Martha heard a buzz of conversation which she could not understand.

At the door, Phil found a stranger standing there whom he could not recall ever meeting before.

"Pastor George Browning of the Sheepfold Fellowship," the large bearded figure beamed. "Very pleased to meet you, my brother."

"Oh, I . . ." Phil stammered.

"I just heard from James Frame about your dear wife's sickness. James as you know is a Civil Servant and he was advising me about tax matters when he mentioned your wife's condition. Immediately the Lord spoke to me and confirmed that I should come here at once and pray for your wife's healing! God is able! Hallelujah!"

Phil was taken aback by the sudden appearance of this pastor. Nevertheless he decided that as the pastor had made the effort to visit them, he should be invited in.

Phil was still wincing somewhat at the volume of Pastor Browning's announcement when Gwen cried out, "Who is it, Phil?"

"Er, it's umm . . . it's Pastor Browning. He's come to see you, dear. We'll maybe come through for a moment if that's all right."

Gwen was not feeling like receiving visitors, but she agreed to a brief visit.

Pastor Browning entered the bedroom with a gushing display of emotion. Sitting quietly at Gwen's bedside, Martha eyed him with a degree of suspicion.

"The Lord told me to come and lay hands on you for recovery, my dear sister, and we're going to believe together for your healing," George asserted confidently.

Martha cringed within as he went on pompously.

"We all know from the Scripture that healing is in the atonement and that our Savior was the great sickness-bearer, as well as sin-bearer of His people." Pastor George was gaining momentum now and at this point he broke into unintelligible utterances which greatly surprised and disturbed those gathered. Laying hands on Gwen he rebuked the cancer in the Lord's name and commanded it to come out of her at that very instant.

After a few more moments of speaking in tongues he calmed down somewhat and pronounced Gwen healed, if she should continue to have faith.

A general air of confusion—hope mixed with incredulity and uncertainty—prevailed as the pastor made his exit. He promised to continue to pray and to return again soon to see the results of the day's labors.

Gwen was flushed and excitable as she grasped Phil's hand and murmured, "I do hope that I can keep up the faith that I've been healed. Isn't it wonderful that the Lord should send that man to us just at this time of need?"

Phil wasn't so sure, but not wanting to discourage his wife in any way or display his own lack of faith, he agreed that it was wonderful indeed.

Martha rose to go, saying that it was late and she had to be getting back home.

"So what did you think of it, Martha?" Phil added as they got to the front door, out of earshot of Gwen.

"I think, dear brother, that you should get in touch with Alan as soon as possible and tell him about this visit," Martha replied tersely.

This stunned Phil, but he said, "Yes, yes, I suppose I should. It is all rather mystifying to me, and I wouldn't want to demonstrate unbelief in this situation and hinder any miracle taking place."

He bid Martha goodnight as she walked toward the bus stop with a remarkably determined step for an octogenarian!

* * *

James Frame and Roger Drury and their wives, Jean and Monica, had decided to visit the Wilsons on Wednesday evening. This provided them with an excuse should anyone ask why they were not at the prayer meeting. After exchanging pleasantries and expressing regret about Gwen's condition, the underlying reason for their visit then became apparent.

"We don't want to upset you folks at this time," James began, "but we have been talking to several of the members and they are all anxious to get this matter regarding Alan Kerr resolved quickly."

Phil looked nervously at Gwen.

126

Roger Drury noticed and he quickly added, "Now we understand that you have enough to worry about at this particular juncture without concerning yourselves about the church's difficulties, too. However, we just thought that it would be good to know that you will support us when we raise the matter officially."

James Frame nodded agreement with Roger's statement.

Gwen tried to say something but was obviously distressed, and Phil spluttered a little shamefacedly, "Er, you see, we, well, with all this trouble that's come upon us we don't want to get involved just now in any controversy. What with Gwen's condition and all that."

A heavy silence fell across the room. Finally, Monica said, "Of course we don't expect you and Gwen to come to the meeting when it's arranged, but just to know that we have your support is all we want.

She looked around at the others and they gave her smiles of acquiescence.

"Well, we won't disturb you any more at this time," James Frame said, rising to go. "Just wanted to know that we could count on your support in trying to save the church from this takeover bid by *these people* at this time."

The two couples took their leave without any recourse to prayer or further expression of sympathy for Gwen's condition.

* * *

Ron had arranged to meet Jack Kemp for lunch and then go to the book shop to see if there were any new books that might attract their attention. Besides, they loved to have fellowship with the two old sisters who always made them feel so welcome.

"Going to the prayer meeting tonight, sisters?" Ron asked banteringly.

"Now you know the answer to that," Mrs. Shearer replied, wagging her finger at him in mock rebuke. "I've a good mind not to show you something that might be of considerable interest to you."

Jack joined in at this point saying, "He doesn't deserve your kindness toward him, Mrs. Shearer!"

"What's all this about?" Ron protested.

Mrs. Shearer went into the back room and later emerged with another paperback in her hand. Ron saw that it was much thicker than the Bounds paperbacks and he and Jack crowded round her to catch a glimpse of the title, *Only a Prayer Meeting* by C. H. Spurgeon.

They both said it aloud at the same time as they almost snatched it out of Mrs. Shearer's hand.

"Great!" Ron said excitedly. "I'd like to have it. How much is it?"

"I'm not sure yet," Mrs. Shearer said, secretly pleased that the young men could be excited about a volume on prayer. "These books are published in America and I haven't worked out the exchange rate yet."

"But . . ." she paused for dramatic effect and said mischievously, "it will be very expensive!"

"Never mind," Ron responded, "I want to have it anyway."

"You just take it, dear, and I'll let you know the price the next time you drop into the shop."

"Oh, thanks," Ron said gratefully, as he and Jack began to peruse the list of chapter contents.

"Listen to this," Ron addressed the company, for Martha had come from the back room curious about the hubbub in the shop. "Spurgeon says, 'Fasten your grips, first on the Lord

Jesus Christ,' then he goes on saying, 'Fasten on the doctrines of the Gospel, then on the service which God has given you to do.' He continues further by saying, 'Fasten your grips on the Cross and upon one another. And all of this we can do by prayer and . . .'"

"Hey! What's going on here?" Alan's voice cut in to Ron's recitation.

Due to the excitement Ron was generating over his recent acquisition, they had not noticed him come in.

"It's this latest book I've just bought, Alan. Have you read it?"

Alan took it from Ron's hand and shook his head. "No," he said deliberately as he turned several of the pages, "but I have heard of it, and it looks like it would be good sound material. Well, anything Spurgeon writes generally is, isn't it?"

"Can't argue with that," Jack said authoritatively.

Ron and Jack suddenly realized that it was time to return to their work. Alan and the two old ladies retired to the back room for a cup of tea and a chat.

"I'm worried about it all, Alan," Martha said, as Mrs. Shearer poured the tea.

"Tell me exactly what this brother said and did," Alan asked gently.

"Well, it was his whole manner that distressed me. It was kind of intimidating. I think that he has left poor Phil and Gwen in a state of confusion. They don't need that kind of agitation with all the difficulties they have at present."

"I'm sure that the pastor meant well, although we might not agree with his interpretation of Scripture," Alan replied. "However, I think that I should drop in and see the Wilsons this afternoon."

"Oh, yes. Do that," Martha said with some relief in her

voice. "I'm so glad that you came in just now because I was going to phone you about this whole matter later today."

* * *

Alan was seated in the Wilson's front room and was listening to their account of Pastor Browning's visit and his pronouncement that Gwen would be healed if she continued believing. He sighed deeply within himself. He had faced this dilemma on many occasions and had often witnessed the sad results that inevitably follow this kind of teaching. How he sincerely wished such a gift of healing was his and he could restore Gwen to health and fitness. He thought of the teeming streets of Hyderabad in India, and how many times he had seen people die like flies by the side of the road. How he longed that those like Pastor Browning would visit such locations and heal multitudes who had no recourse to medical facilities.

"What a blessing," he continued to think, "if we could get the great faith healers away from their TV productions and out into the casualty departments of our city hospitals."

Gwen's anxious inquiry jolted Alan from his reverie.

"Do you really think I've been healed, Alan?" she asked, with an expectant note in her voice that he hated to deflate.

"These things are in the Lord's hands," he said compassionately.

Phil interjected with a forthright question asking, "Is it true what that man said about healing being in the atonement and that every Christian will be healed if they believe for it and claim it?"

Alan wished that he was somewhere far off at that very moment. He sensed that the Wilsons were heading for that place where they would eventually conclude that with healing being available and them not receiving, then the fault must logically be either theirs or God's. This ultimately was the cleft stick to which such teaching brought earnest souls.

Alan began as gently as he could to address the question posed by the Wilsons. "I want to make it clear that I believe that God heals people today. However, I must also say that I do not believe that the Bible teaches that healing is in the atonement. Neither do I believe that it teaches that any persons have the gift of healing as the Apostles had in the early church period."

Alan paused and looked closely at Gwen and Phil, trying to gauge the effect that this pronouncement was having on them. He was encouraged to see they were listening with rapt attention to his words.

"I read recently in a book by a great theologian[59] that, 'atonement can only be made for fault.'" Alan continued, "Then are Pastor Browning and those who believe as he does suggesting that sickness is a fault for which we are responsible and for which atonement can be made?"

"Well, I certainly hope not," Phil said decidedly.

"I don't think that any of us could reasonably deny that God has not excluded sin from His will or purpose for His people. So why should sickness be a special case?" Alan stood up and, moving to Gwen's bedside, said gently, "I think we will find that there are just as many Christians sick and suffering in Pastor Browning's group and those of like persuasion, as there are in any other branch of Christianity."

"Yes, I do believe you're right," Gwen said seriously. "And you know, Alan, it is a relief in a way to know that we don't have to be struggling to try and achieve a pinnacle of acceptability by our own will power. But why then do you think that the Lord has allowed me to be stricken with this cancer?"

"I don't think that any of us are privy to that kind of information, Gwen. In the sovereignty of God, He does allow His people to be sick. It cannot be denied that as the First Cause of all things He has made some babies to be born with abnormalities or deformities. Some are born deaf and dumb or blind. Why God has allowed this particular infirmity to come upon you at this time, I cannot tell."

"I suppose it's something like what happened to Job," Phil said. "There didn't seem to be much reason for that, naturally speaking, did there?"

"No, I guess not," Alan said wryly. "That case is probably the classic example of a man having to submit to the sovereign disposal of God toward him with very little apparent understanding of the terrible calamity. On the other hand, however, we have the narrative in Isaiah 38 where Hezekiah was sick, close to death, and he besought the Lord with fervent intercession for healing. Remember how God granted his request, but he also demanded through the prophet Isaiah that a cake of figs be applied to the boil so that Hezekiah might recover. In other words, the lesson for us from the incident is simply, pray for healing but utilize medical means like doctors, medicines, surgery, and the like."

Alan could not help feeling elated that in spite of the Wilsons' awful dilemma, he saw a marked difference in their attitude and spiritual responses. He almost felt convicted that he was feeling like this in the midst of Gwen's obvious discomfort and terminal condition. But, there was no denying that she was a totally different woman from the one who had so recently been associated with those who came to demand his removal as interim pastor.

After a brief word of prayer and a word of assurance to the Wilsons that the church would uphold them in their trying and painful time, Alan turned to leave. Suddenly Gwen

132

half rose from the bed and said with a degree of emotion that startled Alan, "I just want you to know how very much I appreciate you calling and your interest in both Phil and me. Now I also know that you have been very kind not to mention that the Bible also has something to say about how sin can induce disease and . . ."

Alan sought to interrupt Gwen, but she continued.

"No, Alan, I know that you don't want to infer that I am in this condition because of sin, but I definitely want you to pray that the Lord will forgive me for my opposing you. I am convinced now that it *is* the Lord's will for you to be appointed pastor."

Gwen sank back into the pillows, her face flushed from the exertion of speaking. Looking toward Phil she saw him nod decisively in agreement. Alan was not normally given to demonstrative emotionalism, but he felt a lump arise in his throat and tears start in his eyes at this unexpected declaration of support. He was in no state to elaborate further concerning the thought raised by Gwen that sickness could come as chastening for sin, or at times from Satan himself, or for acts of disobedience.

"I'll have to be going now," Alan said in a soft farewell. "But I promise to come back before too long."

He was soon out in the chill of the winter afternoon with a surrealistic sense of being in another dimension as he fought in his mind to bring the day's events into some kind of logical perspective. He knew the Wilsons would never be the same again and that the Lord was irrevocably bringing the jigsaw puzzle of events concerning the church into place. "Who can but wonder," he pondered as he made his way through the misty cold breeze, "at the wonderful way that God can bring good out of apparent total disaster?"

14

Heart trembling is not always a sign of unbelief

"Bill Morgan has been trying to contact you. He's phoned here several times."

Alan was just about to lift the receiver and call Bill when the phone rang again.

"Bill?" Alan said quizzically. "Carol tells me that you've been trying to get hold of me all afternoon."

"Yes, I have," Bill replied, sounding a bit worried. "We have to meet as soon as possible."

"Why? What's wrong?" Alan asked. Now *his* voice betrayed a little anxiety.

"Oh no, not that," Alan replied as Bill began to unfold what was troubling him.

* * *

As Bill hurriedly finished his evening meal he was obviously disturbed. "I contacted Alan just as soon as I received the letter," he said to Ruth. "You know, I can hardly believe that James Frame would do something so deceitful. We've been deacons together for years, yet he deliberately went behind my back and arranged this meeting."

"Well, I don't think it will prosper if it is done in such a hole-in-a-corner way," Ruth said.

"You're right. But it still comes as something of a shock when a fellow Christian treats you in such a way. I'd best be off because I said I would meet Alan at his home at 7:30 p.m."

* * *

Bill and Alan seated themselves in Alan's front room before a cheery gas fire and they spread out the letter before them.

"I'm not surprised at all," Alan said ruefully. "But we could do without this trouble at this particular time, especially since the Wilsons are having such difficulties."

"Never is a convenient time for these things I suppose," Bill said wearily. "But the question is, what do you think we should do about it?"

"I think that we should just let them go ahead with the meeting. Let's face it, they will whether we agree or not. The fact that they have not even consulted you as the other deacon indicates the lack of respect they have for the church constitution. If you add their disinterest in Scriptural practice and even lack of common courtesy, then what can you do?"

"But," Alan continued, "sadly when people get the bit between their teeth and begin to operate in the flesh rather than the Spirit, then the Word of God no longer commands any restraint or authority over them. This is one of the fruits of backsliding I regret to say."

"At least we have one prayer meeting night before next Wednesday," Bill exclaimed. "And it's unlikely that we'll see many of the opposition there because they are not given to attending prayer meetings. However, the nucleus who have genuine concern for the glory of God and the unity and preservation of the church will be there to pray for this issue."

"If you're not in a great hurry to get off, Bill, we can spend a little time ourselves now committing the situation to God's hand and seeking His wisdom."

* * *

At lunch time on Wednesday Ron and Jack had excitedly made their way to the book shop. Now they were gathered in the little back room and, having brought sandwiches with them, were eating lunch with the two old sisters, who as usual had made them a cup of tea.

"I cannot believe it," Ron exploded indignantly and rather animatedly.

"I felt exactly the same when I received mine," Jack said, as he munched a sandwich.

"What do you sisters make of it?" Ron inquired. "You did get one, didn't you?"

"Yes, we did, Ron," Mrs. Shearer said sadly. "And we took it to the Lord in prayer asking Him to give us wisdom in the matter."

"Wisdom?" Ron responded angrily. "Wisdom? These people should be thrown out of the church. They're nothing but troublemakers."

"We know how you feel, dear," Martha said gently. "But we must not let our feelings run away with us in such situations."

"What then do you suggest that we do?" Ron asked in exasperation.

"It doesn't seem like a very Christian act to me," Jack ventured, looking to Ron for approval.

"Now then," Mrs. Shearer spoke softly, "let's just look at what the letter says again."

The offending letter sent by James Frame purported to speak on behalf of a large number of church members. It gave notice of a special business meeting on the following Wednesday evening to discuss the church's future and the necessity of a speedy appointment of an *official* pastor.

Not recognizing Alan as acting pastor and feeling that he had considerable support in the church, James Frame had not consulted with Bill Morgan concerning the special meeting.

"I say that we should get organized," Ron said heatedly. "We ought to lobby people and persuade then just as they do at the Houses of Parliament. We know that many of these rebels are spineless waverers with no real convictions. They need someone to point them in the right direction."

"Did you glean this strategy from Mr. Bounds' books, Ron?" Martha asked impishly as she glanced up from her knitting.

She had been sitting quietly, listening to the debate while clicking away at an unrecognizable garment that was beginning to take form on her knitting needles.

Ron flushed at this barb and blustered out an incoherent remark before Mrs. Shearer interjected quietly. "This is where knowledge has to be outworked practically. I'm sure that we are all very impressed by good books at various times in our lives, but true understanding only comes when our wills are resolved to do the right thing."

Jack nodded in agreement, "Mrs. Shearer's right, Ron. It's in times like these that we have to practice those things which have inspired us in the Bible, or any book we have read."

"I guess you're right," Ron said somewhat shamefacedly.

"It all boils down to practicing what you preach, eh? But these people do aggravate you all the same. However, what *are* we going to do about the situation?"

* * *

"Yes, Roger," James Frame said as he answered the phone. "A meeting you say? Yes, I think that it would be a good idea in view of the present trouble."

"I've got something to bring for your consideration, James," Roger went on. "Why don't we get a few of the folks together and discuss things?"

"Sounds good to me," James Frame replied. "I know that James Leonard would like to be present and certainly one or two of the other men."

They decided to arrange a meeting just for the men on Friday evening.

* * *

James Frame had managed to contact about a dozen men who promised to come to the meeting in his home to discuss the forthcoming Wednesday confrontation in the church. James was a little disappointed to note, as his sitting room began to fill up, that Phil Wilson was absent. Roger Drury, James Leonard, and Albert Higgins were all seated and talking animatedly to one another. There were several in attendance who would fiercely affirm themselves to be members in good standing though they appeared to be unaware that the church met on any occasion other than Sunday mornings, except for business meetings of course. They were all ensconced comfortably, manifesting a lively anticipation and relish for the agenda.

James Frame rose, and clearing his throat, announced the meeting open. He welcomed those assembled, expressed his great regret at having to convene such a gathering, and said, "In view of the extreme seriousness of the situation, I felt it necessary to seek wise, experienced, impartial counsel to help us at this time. To this end we are going to have a visitor preside over our discussions and I expect his arrival at any moment."

This announcement sparked a buzz of conversation as the men speculated who the mystery visitor might be. Just then the doorbell rang and James, with a slight smirk on his face perceptible only to a keen onlooker, excused himself to answer it.

The others waited expectantly as they tried to recognize the muffled voice in the hallway.

James entered the room first and announced triumphantly, "Gentlemen, I'm sure that you will be delighted as I am to welcome again into our midst, our dear brother, Pastor Andrew Paterson."

James could hardly conceal his smug sense of satisfaction as he announced to the assembled members the arrival of Pastor Paterson.

"We're grateful to our Brother Andrew for sparing us his valuable time and showing concern for the state of our church in these days of crisis," James intoned pompously and fatuously. This seemed to escape the attention of the hearers, and the flattery had a tranquilizing effect on Andrew, rendering him quite amenable to the hypocrisy and deception surrounding the meeting.

"Let's call the meeting to order," James boomed loudly. "You all know why we're gathered here tonight. I need hardly remind you that we're agreed that no one is going to wrest the church from us and impose his will on us arbitrarily."

140

He looked around for approval of his opening remarks and was gratified with several murmurs of agreement. "Now if you have any questions or suggestions, this is the time to voice them." He sat down and, peering over his half spectacles, invited comments.

James Leonard and Roger Drury both began to speak at the same time, but Roger eventually withdrew as James Leonard pressed on, oblivious to anyone else speaking.

"I feel strongly about what these people are trying to do, and some of them have been in the church for no length of time. My question is, do we have sufficient votes to defeat them on Wednesday?"

"Good point, good point," James Frame nodded sagaciously. "We'll have to make sure that we all get to the meeting on Wednesday and bring others of like mind with us."

Roger Drury interrupted, "We *never* had this trouble when our Brother Andrew was pastor." Another murmur of approval followed this remark. "I wonder if he could give us any advice as to how we should tackle this meeting. . . ." He paused dramatically before continuing, "Constitutionally, so to speak."

"Er . . . well," Andrew blustered, obviously unprepared for such a direct question. "Eh . . ." he cleared his throat again and then continued uncertainly. "First, let me thank you all for inviting me here tonight. Like yourselves, I am naturally concerned about any disturbances or divisions in God's church. In addition to this, Earlton Baptist Church was my former charge where I spent many happy years."

He tacked this latter statement on, almost as an after thought, but it did have the guaranteed effect of warming the audience toward him.

"Of course I don't want to interfere in the affairs of what to me is now *another* church. I would just advise that if you

141

would present your case in a brotherly way, I'm sure that you'll be able to come to an amicable solution."

He appeared to have finished his statement when he hurriedly added what seemed suspiciously like another after-thought. "Let us all remember that whatever we do, we must try and do it for the glory of God!"

James Frame eventually concluded the meeting after a lengthy and somewhat heated discussion more akin to a po-litical pressure group than a group of professing Christians. Andrew was asked to sanctify the meeting with prayer, in which he asked God to help them all in their quest of preserv-ing the church. After parting exchanges, the men retired to prepare for the upcoming battle. The total absence of any ref-erence to the Word of God or any serious prayer in relation to the event appeared to be of little concern to any of them. Andrew was just a little uneasy about some of these aspects as he made his way home, but he consoled himself that he was well out of the situation.

15

I don't know exactly what to pray for

"These Sunday morning services are a bit of an ordeal even though I've tried to put this impending business meeting out of my mind," Alan pondered, as he prepared to go to church.

James Frame and his supporters were together mainly in the back rows of the church. Alan could sense their hostility and if he had not made the effort to shake hands at the conclusion of the service, they would have skulked out without saying a word to him. Alan noticed that James Leonard, a Sunday-only member, was hanging around the exit looking toward him. Alan had very little previous contact with him because of his peripheral allegiance to the church, but he could see by the clouded look on James Leonard's face that something was troubling him. As Alan approached him, Leonard, a burly short man with reddish, fair hair now going bald, spoke to him.

"I'd like to see you for a minute," he said brusquely in belligerence and rudeness.

Alan ignored the tone of Leonard's voice and calmly asked, "Shall we go into the office?"

"Yes, it won't take a minute for what I want to say,"

Leonard replied, his countenance still clouded and unfriendly. Once inside the office, Alan invited him to take a seat and state his business.

"I'm not a man given to any fancy talking, so I'll come straight to the point if you don't mind," he said.

Alan listened intently, looking him straight in the eye, which seemed to disconcert him a little.

"There would be no need for this meeting if you adopted a more reasonable and Christian attitude in this dispute," Leonard said aggressively.

"I'm not sure that I understand you," Alan said quietly.

"Oh, you understand me perfectly well," Leonard responded. "If you had any real concern for this church, you would get out and leave us members in peace like we had before you arrived on the scene."

"Well, thank you for your comments," Alan said, "but I think it would be better for us to leave the members to decide these issues on Wednesday. After all, maybe you have forgotten that it was Mr. Frame and his supporters who demanded this meeting in the first place."

As Alan ushered him from the office, Leonard muttered something about "people professing to be Christians who had no love for their fellow members."

When Alan arrived home, Carol was wondering what had detained him at church. "I saw that fellow Leonard waiting to speak to you, so I and the children just made our way home."

"Yes, that's what kept me back. And to tell you the truth, I think it's the first conversation I've had with the man since we arrived here."

"I guess it was more trouble," Carol said resignedly.

"What else?" Alan asked with a touch of humor. "Whenever it rains, it pours!"

144

Carol brought in a tray to set the table for dinner and they changed the subject as the children joined them.

Later, Alan sat back in his old armchair while Carol tidied the kitchen. He found his heart trembling slightly as he thought of the coming Wednesday.

"But heart trembling is not always a sign of unbelief," he mused. "I trust in this case that it is a conscious recognition of weakness and unworthiness. I'm not foolish enough to think," he continued to ponder, "that I am the *goody* and James Frame and the others are the *baddies*. I've probably made my contribution to the situation by lack of wisdom and discernment. However, the Lord has special regard for those who look to Him unashamedly for help, and my experiences testify that such an attitude invariably brings, in His appointed time, unique manifestations of His presence and help."[60]

* * *

"I have to be honest and say that I'm glad and relieved that the Sunday services are over," Alan thought. "It's just tragic that I, or anyone else, as a Christian should have to dread going to church to worship the Lord. This ought to be a joy for us."

James Frame and his backers were occupying their back rows in the church. They had been huddled together as if trying to derive mutual strength from their physical closeness.

"What a sullen, silent opposition emanated from them as I preached. It's enough to sadden and depress anyone," Alan said to himself.

"What probably is depressing me more is that a few who are now congregated with the opposition apparently once ran well. Now their backslidden hearts have naturally gravitated to those of similar disposition."

145

Alan felt a shudder of apprehension go through him as he marveled at the restraint of grace that reigns in a true believer's heart. He was suddenly overjoyed that, by sovereign grace, he had been restrained from ever preferring association with backsliders no matter how disappointed he'd been with his own spiritual walk or how depressed he'd been by the conduct of others. Had these poor deluded souls ever known the touch of that grace which they seemed so resolutely determined to ignore?

Alan's mind flashed back in the middle of this contemplation to a passage in a book that he had recently read. It was written by the pastor of a foremost church among English dissenters in the 18th century. Speaking of those deceived persons who attempt to join grace and works together to accomplish a given end, with works usually predominating, the pastor wrote:

> However high their pretenses to holiness, it is plain from the Word of God, and it may in some degree appear from the nature of the thing, that they take an effectual way to ruin their souls forever, except that very grace prevent, of which they have such false and corrupt ideas. For divine grace disdains to be assisted in the performance of that work which peculiarly belongs to itself, or by the poor, imperfect performances of men. Attempts to complete what grace begins, betray our pride and offend the Lord, but cannot promote our spiritual interest.[61]

"I can't help feeling a degree of compassion for James Frame and his cronies though," Alan thought. "It's only God's grace that has prevented me from manifesting the same tendencies."

He was silently beseeching God to keep him totally dependent on grace when Bill broke into his thoughts.

"Alan, could I have a quick word with you?"

"Sure," Alan responded warmly, "let's go into the office."

Seated in the vestry Bill quickly came to the point.

"It's this meeting on Wednesday, Alan," he said shaking his head wearily. "It's been preying on my mind because I don't want to see a split in the church. On the other hand, I can't see it being avoided if we are going to be faithful to a biblical position."

"Listen, Bill," Alan said earnestly, "if our motives are right, we've nothing to fear. Let's summarize our motives like this. I jotted down these points to clarify them in my mind for Wednesday. If they don't represent our position in any way, feel free to say so."

Alan then listed his main thoughts:

1. A desire to uphold biblical practice and principle
2. A resolution to maintain the unity of the saints at all costs
3. A genuine attempt to rouse the saints to proper praying

Just before they parted, Alan suggested to Bill that it would be beneficial if they could gather the brethren together on Tuesday evening to pray. "This is where the battle is going to be won, I think. Don't you?"

"The way we've been praying, I can't see much hope for us," Bill said disconsolately.

"It's not eloquence, Bill, or our knowledge of theology primarily. It's our hearts, our motives, God with us—that's what will carry the day!" Alan responded.

"You're right," Bill sighed wearily. "I'll contact the men and we can meet at my house, if you like, on Tuesday evening around 7:30."

* * *

147

As Alan, Carol, and the family made their way home from the service, Carol noticed that Alan was pre-occupied and silent.

"Something on your mind?" she asked, guessing that it had to do with the forthcoming meeting on Wednesday.

"You know me too well, Carol, for me to hide anything from you, eh?" he said with a faint grimace.

Settled at home and enjoying peace and quietness after the children had gone to bed, Alan looked somberly at Carol as he said, "I've been thinking a lot about the terrible lack of praying people in the congregation. Even those who are supportive of the ministry are sadly deficient in the realm of intercession. However, one cheering thought did come to me as I recalled the two old sisters. They, at least, are strongly behind my efforts to motivate the church. And, *they* certainly don't fall into the category of those who are strangers to intercession."

"Strangely, I'm encouraged," Carol retorted, "I've noticed that you are showing more of a burden for the lack of spirituality and praying in the church than you are for the coming meeting."

"I'm quietly confident," Alan said, "that God will deal with the dissenters in mercy, but the future of the church lies in it's being directed in spiritual channels, primarily in prayer."

He let his mind drift back to the last prayer meeting and groaned inwardly as he thought of the terrible lack of direction and the cold, wandering, aimless nature of most of the utterances.

"Why do those who are the least gifted in public utterance often pray the longest? Why are there more points in some people's prayers than there are on a porcupine? Fervency, accuracy, brevity! I must get this home to them or perish in the attempt!" Alan was surprised at the intensity of

148

his thoughts.

"It's getting late, Alan. Time we were off to bed," Carol said a trifle wearily.

Alan suddenly became aware that his hands were clenched tightly, the knuckles showing white with the power of his concentration.

"You know," he said just before dropping off to sleep, "I must confess that I would love to know what went on at that meeting in James Frame's house last Friday."

"You may never know, dear," Carol answered sleepily. "So you may as well forget about it. Anyway, I don't think it would be anything to get excited about."

* * *

"Alan, I know this is Monday morning, but I still think you should attempt to shake off the blues."

"Yes, yes, Carol," Alan replied with a touch of exasperation. "But I'm still mighty curious regarding that meeting at James Frame's house last Friday. I can't seem to get it out of my mind. From the cold and hostile attitude the rebels displayed yesterday at the church, I reckon they are still bent on trouble for Wednesday. Anyway I had better get down to serious praying about the meeting tomorrow at Bill's house and the meeting on Wednesday at the church."

"Before you go to your study, Alan, will you replace that plug on my toaster, please? It's dangerous and I've asked you to do it several times already this past week."

Alan attempted several times to get into his study to pray about these crucial issues before he finally made it. After he completed the chore for Carol, the phone rang and he had to answer a couple of questions from Bill about the upcoming meeting in his home. With a sigh of relief he had just gotten

149

to the door of his study when the front doorbell rang. Muttering under his breath Alan opened the door and was confronted by a man from the electric company. He wanted to read the electric meter! Finally Alan reached his study, grimly determined that he would remain there, even if the house fell down!

Alan realized that he had to apply to himself the principles and discipline that he'd begun to teach the church regarding prayer. Although the problems of the church were very pressing, he still found it hard to stop wandering thoughts from seducing him from the task at hand.

"First, I need to be definite. This is no time for generalizations, vagueness, or rambling around," he thought. "Second, my desperate need is wisdom." So quoting James 1:5,6, he besought the Lord earnestly for wisdom from above for the forthcoming meetings.

"Again, I'm conscious that I don't know exactly *what* to pray for because the deep needs I feel in this situation are not easily expressed."

He found himself earnestly quoting Romans 8:26,27 and pleading for the assistance of the Holy Spirit. As Alan continued in his intercessions, he felt a distinct impression conveyed by his conscience that God was asking him if he *truly* wanted his prayers answered. It dawned upon him gradually that a specific answer such as he was requesting could bring many problems and difficulties. There was a need for self-sacrifice, which he had not properly considered before now. Because of the upheaval that would follow the business meeting if the dissidents won the day, it would probably be impossible for those who opposed them to remain in the church. This was certainly a matter for sober consideration. On the other hand, there was the mammoth task which would require unstinted devotion and dedication if the faithful won the day and if the church was then to be established in a viable biblical pattern.

"Are my prayers nothing more than an affront to God?"

These thoughts pummeled Alan's mind as he continued to wrestle and pray. The more he contemplated the sacrifices that pastoring this church would force upon him and his family life, the less attractive the office seemed to be. The violent opposition from supposed fellow Christians to any application of spiritual truths, the lack of any spare time for himself or his family—thoughts of these sacrifices assailed him with doubts as to the validity of his piety. In prayer he was discovering the reality of the objects of his intercessions assumed a more realistic perspective and that they lost some of the attraction that adorned them when viewed from a more earthly distance.

Alan paused in his intercession and thought, "Gone forever are any romantic or egotistical notions about the pastorate. Wrestling with issues becomes wrestling between God and me over my personal willingness to sacrifice much of that with which I'm not certain I'm really willing to part.

"A very good devotee may be a very dishonest suppliant. When he leaves the height of meditative abstraction, and, as we say in our Saxon phrase, *comes to himself*, he may find that his true character, his real self, is no petitioner at all. His devotions have been but illusions. He has been acting a pantomime. He has not really desired that God would give heed to him for any other purpose than to give him an hour of pleasurable devotional excitement. That the objects of his prayer should actually be wrought into his own consciousness is by no means the thing he has been thinking of, and is the last thing he is ready just now to wish for."[62]

151

16

Ye have not, because ye ask not

"I'd better hurry," Ron reminded himself, "because I've arranged to meet Jack and Tim Robson at the cafe for lunch."

Ron had been impressed with Tim's apparent growth in spiritual matters and the enthusiasm he had shown in reading several books that Ron had passed on to him. Tim was an English teacher at the local school, so Ron was encouraged that he had been quite appreciative in receiving the literature.

Seated at the table having lunch, Jack expressed his concern regarding the impending business meeting on Wednesday.

"Well, we're going to have the opportunity to pray about it at Bill's house tonight," Ron responded.

"I've not had much experience of business meetings," Tim said, "because as a relatively new Christian I haven't attended any."

"I haven't been to many either," Jack chipped in, "and I can't say I'm too disappointed about it."

"Oh, come on, they're not as bad as that," Ron said laughingly. Then as a kind of afterthought he said half to himself, "But I guess this one could be different."

"You know, Ron," Tim began, "I really am finding that

153

book I'm reading, *A Guide to Fervent Prayer,*[63] to be most enlightening.

He quoted several passages almost as if he had memorized the book.

Ron and Jack were quite impressed.

However, Ron had one nagging thought in his mind that continued to plague him. "Why," he thought, "when Tim has such enthusiasm for books like this and for discussions on prayer—why is it we don't hear his voice in the prayer meeting?"

The time had arrived for them to return to work. They parted, agreeing to see each other later at Bill's house for the special session of prayer.

Just after 7:30 p.m. the men began to arrive at Bill's house for the prayer meeting. Alan deeply regretted the them-and-us dichotomy which was already evident in the church. Although he feared an even greater schism, he felt that the need of intercession now heavily outweighed the possibility of this meeting leading to further division.

"I want to welcome you all for coming," Bill greeted the men. "Now I know it's a bit crowded for twenty of us in here; however, I trust it won't be too uncomfortable."

Indeed they were overcrowded, but any feelings of discomfort were offset by a joyful attitude over the good attendance. Bill and Alan knew that if it had been open to the sisters as well, the ranks would have been swollen considerably, so they were encouraged by the response and serious attitude that prevailed.

Alan rose in the crowded room to address the men. "Friends, I want to remind you of our grave need and compelling dependence upon God for his intervention at this time. I make no apology for reminding you once again of these principles."

154

Methodically, Alan began to cite the principles of effective prayer, "Brevity: predominantly until we have cultivated the art of prayer. Accuracy and definiteness: we have our Master's example of this in John 17. And, fervency: praying with heart and burden."

Alan then got down on his knees and led in prayer.

After a considerable time lapse, Bill was next to pray. He started well enough, but was soon entangled in generalizations. It was as if, after asking God to help in this crisis, he did not have anything specific to request. He reminded the Lord of his lengthy service in the church and the many difficulties he'd experienced in the past. Grappling somewhat to find inspiration to continue, Bill utilized the title "Lord" as a comma, inserting it after every phrase.

Alan found himself dreading the punctuation.

Bill was unaware of his denigrating God's name in this way and he finally ground to a halt. Sadly, by no stretch of the imagination could he have been accused of *asking* God for anything! The text suddenly leapt to Alan's mind, "Ye have not, because ye ask not."[64]

"Dear God, please help us in this situation," Jack Kemp eventually broke in after another stony silence. Again, he was sincere, but he displayed little burden or direction. His low-key style did nothing to arouse the brethren from the torpor that was settling upon them.

Alan thought, "I'm aware that God can hear the merest sigh and even read the heart and know every unspoken word, but this is mere repetition."

After much lamenting of his spiritual condition and the protracted listing to the Almighty of His many attributes, Jack mercifully fell silent, which few of those present regretted.

At this juncture Ron decided things needed to be taken in hand.

155

"Lord, you know that we are greatly lacking in fervency and energy." He swept in with a loud voice which disturbed and even alarmed several who had drifted into a restful state. Ron was determined and not at all excited by what had gone before. His frustration caused him to offend the brethren when he began to rebuke those guilty of sloth and apathy.

Alan sighed within himself, "Ron's frustration is understandable, but it would have better been addressed by more mature and wiser counsel."

Ron's tirade finally exhausted, he suddenly remembered the need to pray for wisdom and assistance for the Wednesday meeting. It savored somewhat of a postscript attached to his vehement displeasure with the nature and progress of the prayer meeting.

Ron was likewise exasperated by his inability to express himself properly. Nevertheless he realized it wasn't just those possessed of youthful zeal like himself that forgot they were addressing the Mighty God and not a fellow man. A degree of sincerity in all the brethren doubtlessly existed, but there was no unity of purpose and consequently little agreement in prayer manifested among the men.

It was obvious to Alan that they all had little experience in praying for anything outside the province of what personally concerned themselves. Although there was nothing wrong with this *per se,* it was far removed from Paul's exhortation to make "supplication for all saints."[65]

After thoughtful consideration and with some reluctance, Alan decided that he would interrupt the proceedings in the interest of the spiritual good of the gathering. He thought it the best time to try and bring correction and teaching when they were actually engaged in activity which he had been assiduously trying to correct for some time now.

He waited until one or two of the men had continued in

much the same pattern before he told the group to take a break. They got up from their knees and, perhaps sensing they were not about to be complimented for their labors, peered at Alan with some uneasiness.

Alan looked around the room and sensed the apprehension of the men as he cleared his throat to speak. He knew he would need courage and compassion in addressing them.

"This prayer meeting graphically demonstrates to us the reality of just what we face in the warfare of prayer. Look at the elements that rage against us to prevent us from fulfilling our duty fervently, effectually, and unselfishly." Alan paused and looked up from the page in the Bible where he was now concentrating. "This verse in James 4:2 came to me with force as we were praying. 'Ye have not, because ye ask not.' It drove me afresh to cry to God, 'Lord, teach me to pray!' We are finding it extremely difficult to get two of us to agree concerning the issues at hand.'"

"Some have asked God for nothing. Others have positively asked amiss. A few have given us no indication of what's on their hearts. They remain strangely silent."

Eddie Carter, a long time church member and an earnest, if uninstructed soul, broke in by saying, "I feel as if we are missing the mark somehow, but I don't know where we are going wrong."

"That's a good way of describing it," Alan replied. "Let me remind you again of our initial exhortation."

He then stressed his three main points:

Brevity: Let us relentlessly seek for quality in our prayers, rather than quantity.
Accuracy: We are rambling all around without making definite or specific requests.
Fervency: We must ask God for a burden so that we can pray with heart in asking.

157

With his head down and in a low voice, Ron said, "I just want to say that I realized as Alan was speaking that my prayers are more inclined to hinder God answering than to incline Him to answer. I'm being totally selfish, and to be perfectly honest, pride and a desire for revenge against those who oppose us have primarily motivated me." He paused and, near to tears, continued, "I ask the Lord to forgive me."

A pregnant silence followed Ron's confession. There was no doubt about its impact on the men.

"Thank you for your honesty, Ron," Alan said soberly. "Don't be discouraged. Helplessness and humility are wonderful assets in the Christian life. They will make our cries to God more effectual. May He bring all of us to such a place tonight. Let's not regard our helplessness as an obstacle to praying. Instead, let us recognize it as an advantage, and let us be grateful to God for any measure of it that He has given us."

Bill Morgan sighed audibly as he said, "These seven small words that Alan has drawn our attention to—'Ye have not, because ye ask not'—are spiritual dynamite!"

"Yes!" Jack Kemp spoke next, "In the light of this, what excuse can we offer for the frozen silences that are so frequent in our meetings?"

"Exactly, Jack," Alan agreed. "Frozen silences are far below the standard of even occasional praying that itself is often merely repetitious. This in turn is still farther below the standard of regular diligent praying which has little heart in it though it be reasonably sincere. But the gradations, if we may use the expression, between the caliber of all of such utterances and actual fervent prayer exhorted in the New Testament seem to me to be immense.

"These seven words contain the secret of the poverty

158

and powerlessness of the average Christian, of the average minister, of the average church. Why is it, many a Christian is asking, that I make such poor progress in my Christian life? Why do I have so little victory over sin? Why do I win so few souls for Christ? Why do I grow so slowly in the likeness of my Lord and Savior Jesus Christ? And God answers in the words of the text—neglect of prayer, 'Ye have not because ye ask not.'"[66]

17

Lord, I must have a word from Thee

Wednesday dawned beautifully. The bright, sunny sky shining through the breakfast room window caught Alan's attention while he and his family ate breakfast. What a glorious sight! That beauty did not last long, however, for soon several dark, ominous-looking rain clouds began to form to the West. Alan wondered if this were an omen of the storm he anticipated at the special meeting that evening.

Alan usually drove Mary and Stephen to school, but this particular morning he had so much on his mind that he asked Carol to do it. He made his way into the back room where he normally prayed when he did not go down to the study at the church. Soon rain was spattering against the window panes and quite a strong wind was beginning to blow.

"I guess we can expect fairly wintry weather in December," Alan mused. This triggered a thought in his mind of how it had been almost two months since they had come home from India. On the other hand, it seemed just like yesterday.

"I don't think I have ever faced so much trauma in any two-month period of my life," Alan pondered. "I'd better get down to serious praying again about the meeting tonight though."

161

* * *

Bill arrived at the office in a disconsolate frame of mind. He hadn't slept well the night before as he had been plagued with dark, brooding forebodings concerning the impending meeting. He just could not get it out of his mind, He was convinced that something terrible was going to happen.

He was still deeply occupied with his mournful thoughts when Ron tapped on the door and breezed in.

"Morning, Bill," he exclaimed in a remarkably cheerful, unconcerned way.

"How can he be so downright carefree on the morning of such a potentially disastrous day?" Bill asked himself.

Bill managed to squeeze out a rough response, "Yes. Good morning, Ron." His tone of voice implied that he was not in the mood for conversation.

Ron had a disarming lack of awareness at times, although on other occasions it could be quite irritating. On this occasion, it was certainly the latter. But, before Bill could express his disinterest in anything outside the province of business, Ron launched into the deep.

"This is it, Bill! James 'Custer' Frame's last stand! I've been praying that God will sort him and his cronies out tonight."

Bill groaned wearily. He was irritated at Ron's youthful indifference and yet he was envious of his apparent disregard for the consequences of the confrontation.

"Ron!" he said sternly. "That is no way to talk about a deacon in the church and those who sincerely believe as James does." But he didn't feel much conviction in his remark.

"Rubbish!" Ron replied with disdain. "He certainly doesn't have my respect. Not the way he has opposed spiri-

162

tual progress in the church. I don't know how he could ever have been appointed a deacon in the first place with his lack of spirituality."

Bill sighed resignedly, "I've got work to do and so have *you*, so let's just get on with it and leave the Lord to undertake in proceedings tonight." Then sarcastically he added, "If you don't mind."

"No, Bill, I'll be off then," Ron said civilly as he departed.

It was around lunch time when Jack Kemp arrived at the office, looking for Ron. He wanted to discuss the coming meeting and form a mutual plan of action if they had to get involved.

"Hi, Alice. Is Ron around?" Jack asked.

Alice looked up from the desk and smiled, "He just went out for a minute. Said he'd be back shortly."

Jack hadn't really noticed Alice much before. Well, not really as a woman. "She has certainly grown up," he thought, "and very nicely, too. She is very attractive!"

Although Alice was not a Christian, she had heard the Gospel from Bill and Ron and she recognized that they were different from most of the other people she knew.

Jack sat down in a chair in the receptionist's office and he began to talk to Alice. Gradually he brought the conversation around to the Gospel and he gently began to witness to her about how he had become a Christian. He was apprehensive that Alice might not be receptive, but she listened quite intently as he spoke.

Just before Ron eventually appeared, Jack, although conscious that he should not enter into any romantic relationship with an unbeliever, finally summoned up the courage to ask Alice if she would like to attend church with him and hear more of the Gospel. "Alan is so much better at explaining these things than I am," he said.

Alice flushed slightly and stammered. "Well, I . . . I'm not sure, but yes, I suppose I could come along this Sunday evening."

The fact was that she had noticed Jack on several occasions when he had come to meet Ron and she had thought that he seemed a nice, decent, respectable boy.

Just then Ron bustled through the doorway. He burst out in his usual tactful way, "Aye, aye, what's going on here?"

It was just a casual remark, but had he been more observant he would surely have noticed the flush that appeared on Alice's cheeks and the degree of consternation on Jack's face.

* * *

James Frame was confidently looking forward to the meeting and was quite assured of the ability of his supporters to carry the day. Like Bill Morgan, James was not concentrating on his work. As he sat at his desk, however, he was not agitated like Bill. Instead he was cool amid scheming, calculating how many might stand with him if there were a narrow vote. He figured it would be a close vote, especially as he wasn't sure about a number who were still undecided. He had phoned a number of people, including Roger Drury. Several, who seldom if ever attended church, nevertheless assured him that they would be there to support his cause.

* * *

Mrs. Shearer had just opened the shop when Martha arrived.

"I think I know why you have come early today, Martha," she said.

"Yes, I thought that we would want to spend extra time in prayer for this evening's meeting. I'm very concerned that things may get out of hand unless the Lord restrains the situation."

"Well, we'll have a cup of tea first, and if the shop is not busy we can spend time before the Lord right away," Mrs. Shearer said warmly.

Alan was on his knees with the Word of God before him. It was his habit to continually read the Word of God from Genesis to Revelation. He had read the Bible through once for every year he had been converted. The particular portion which he was to read this day was Exodus 14.

"I urgently need to hear from thee, Lord, regarding what I should do at this coming business meeting," he prayed.

"Lord, thou knowest I must have a word from Thee regarding what course we should adopt this evening. Please speak, Lord, even from this passage before me!" he continued fervently and with single-mindedness.

He began to read the chapter. It was certainly relevant for the children of Israel were in a real dilemma with the Egyptians. As Alan read the thirteenth verse his attention was powerfully arrested.

"Now what's this," he uttered as he read that the people were to "fear not and stand still." The fourteenth verse really came home to him with tremendous impact, *The Lord shall fight for thee, and ye shall hold your peace.*

"I know that there are explicit promises of Divine guidance and that we can know God's mind for our actions.[67] It could be that this verse in Exodus comes very close to instructing me on the procedure I should adopt at the meeting tonight. Doesn't it presume the necessity of utter dependence upon God and the forsaking of any fleshly means or natural gifts to accomplish the desired result? In view of this I don't feel that I am wresting any Scripture to my own preferred end. The verse certainly appears to encourage the practice of recognized biblical principles and that must be beneficial."[68]

Alan realized that to adopt this strategy would require complete trust in the Lord. It certainly was not the plan that he would have adopted naturally. The more he thought about it, the more he was convinced that God had spoken to him and that he must implement His instructions. After spending time beseeching the Lord to prevent unseemly or carnal display from either side in the dispute, he rose from his knees with a great sense of inner peace and a deep-seated feeling that God was going to work things out without any great assistance from his creatures.

"Above all things, an interpreter of Scripture needs a sound and sober judgment. His mind must be competent to analyze, examine, and compare. He must not allow himself to be influenced by hidden meanings, and spiritualizing processes, and plausible conjectures. He must weigh reasons for and against a given interpretation. He must judge whether his principles are tenable and self-consistent; he must often balance probabilities, reach conclusions with the greatest caution. Such a discriminating judgment may be trained and strengthened, and no pains should be spared to render it a safe and reliable habit of the mind."[69]

Alan had picked up a notebook with notes he had taken at one of the lectures in the Bible College and he wondered if old Professor Johnson would have approved of his hermeneutical principle at this time.

"Well, he's not around to ask," Alan smiled wryly. Nevertheless he was convinced that this plan of action was from the Lord, and that he had sought to implement the main principles which governed sound interpretation.

18

How can a Christian oppose a man of God?

"What!" Bill gasped over the phone to Alan. "Brother, you can't spring this on me at this late hour. I mean, the meeting is due to start in a couple of hours. Alan, I never dreamed that you would not be leading the meeting. I'm no good at public ministry. I . . . er . . . I'm pulverized at the thought. I can't do it. Come on, give me a break!"

Alan cut him short, "Listen, we have no alternative. James Frame will be expecting me to lead this meeting and will have already planned to call this unconstitutional and force me to relinquish the chair publicly. We can't allow him this advantage. This way we can spike his guns and frustrate a few of his carnal plans at least. However, there's another, more important reason. God has convinced me that I must leave this whole matter entirely in His hands."

"Yes, but that surely doesn't mean that you have to be totally passive, does it?"

"Not necessarily, but then on the other hand it may."

Bill groaned heavily at the other end of the phone, "I knew it would come to something like this, something beyond what we can handle."

167

"You're right," Alan said in measured tones. "And does that not suggest to you that the Lord's hand is in all of this, and we need to exercise faith and pray for a solution to be outworked for His glory? Isn't it possible that God has ordered these circumstances to teach us to trust Him more?" He recited how he believed the Lord had spoken concerning the matter and that there was plenty of Scriptural principle to substantiate such a stand.

"Well, I'm not so sure," Bill muttered a little uncertainly.

"You got your Bible handy, Bill?"

"Yes, it's right here on the table."

"Look, we don't have time for any in-depth Bible study at this late hour," Alan retorted. "But turn for a minute to Second Samuel 16. Take a quick look at verses five to fourteen. Abishai was eager to behead Shimei, but I think David had the mind of the Lord. If you quickly turn to chapter 19:16-23, you'll have to agree that David found passivity in this instance paid rich dividends."

Bill sighed deeply again, "Yes, I guess you're right. It's the old story—my faith finds trusting completely in the Lord in these situations difficult because of its emaciated, unexercised condition in the Christian walk. Right, Alan. If I perish, I perish! What is it you want me to do?"

"Good man!" Alan encouraged him. "Now I don't want you to do anything really that we don't feel is for the glory of God, the benefit of the saints, and ultimately helpful for the propagation of the Gospel. Just try and keep the meeting in dignified order, and act as impartially as God will enable you to do. Otherwise, let's leave the outcome to the Lord."

"You had better start praying for me because I'm petrified. Strangely enough, however, I feel that God is going to help me and those of us who have His glory and the church's spiritual welfare at heart."

"Great! We'll be praying for you, Bill. Just remember, we have a mighty, sovereign God who foreknows all things and has foreordained all things."

Alan felt keenly for Bill. He knew that he had sprung a heavy responsibility upon him insofar as Bill's abilities and experience were concerned, but he had to forestall James Frame's strategy which he felt sure was to humiliate him and gain advantage by this for his own cause.

Alan found himself thinking, "I'm not unduly concerned about the possibility of James Frame or his cohorts humiliating me publicly, but rather that any apparent success in the meeting on their part would engender more bravado among the dissenters and make the meeting even more turbulent. Anyway it is firmly in God's hands now, and there is just about time for a final brief spell of intercession before Carol and I set off for the meeting."

* * *

The book shop had closed early on Wednesday afternoon and Mrs. Shearer and Martha had spent considerable time praying for the outcome of the meeting that night. Mrs. Shearer had picked up one of A. W. Pink's books and read excerpts that she thought were relevant to the way the genuine saints should handle the situation.

"I am greatly encouraged, Martha, when I read the comments which Mr. Pink has made regarding God's dealings with the wicked." She hastily added that she was not inferring that James Frame and his supporters were wicked people, but that in their ignorance the Lord could deal with them on the same basic principles as He deals with wicked people.

Martha knew that Mrs. Shearer's comments were not malicious and she listened attentively while busily clicking away at her indefinable knitting garment.

"God sometimes exerts upon the wicked a restraining influence by which they are prevented from doing what they are naturally inclined to do. A striking example of this is seen in Abimilech, King of Gerar, when he sent and took Sarah regarding her as an unmarried woman," Mrs. Shearer explained.

She then reminded Martha of how Joseph's brethren treated him so badly and even conspired to slay him in Genesis 37:18, but God did not allow them to carry out their evil plans.

"God sometimes exerts upon the wicked a softening influence, disposing them contrary to their natural inclinations to do that which will promote His cause,"[70] she remarked.

"I'll have to stop now. Time's running out," Mrs. Shearer said. "It is wonderful though how the Lord has control of all things!" She positively beamed and certainly displayed no apprehension concerning the forthcoming meeting.

Martha stopped her knitting and said, "This is the verse that the Lord has impressed upon me regarding the whole matter. Proverbs 21:1, 'The king's heart is in the hand of the LORD, as the rivers of water: he turneth it whithersoever he will.'"

* * *

James Frame had arranged for several members to pick up any who would support their cause but who did not have transportation to church. This basically applied to a few older members who rarely attended church and who were completely in the dark concerning any of the present issues.

James and his wife Jean set out for the church in good time and he was well satisfied that he had done everything possible to ensure that his cause would prevail. He arrived at the church parking lot just as Bill and Ruth were getting out of their car.

"Just the man I wanted to see," James Frame shouted to Bill. "Can we go into this side room for a moment? There's something I want to speak to you about."

Bill nodded, hoping that James would not notice his nervousness.

"What's on your mind?" Bill asked as casually as he could, belying his inner feelings.

"Just to say that neither I, nor the majority of the members I have spoken to, want Alan Kerr to take any official part in the meeting tonight. After all he—"

Bill interrupted him and curtly said, "He isn't going to."

James stridently pressed the matter further, "I mean we're not having him leading this meeting." His voice rose as he emphasized the word *him*.

"He is not going to," Bill asserted again. Actually he began to strengthen in his resolve as he detected James Frame's obsessive attitude.

"What do you mean, he's not going to," James replied uncertainly and displaying a little trace of confusion.

Bill was beginning to enjoy the encounter and was extremely grateful now for Alan's foresight in the matter.

"James, do you understand plain English?"

"I . . . er . . . Of course I do, but I thought that—"

"Yes, we know what you thought, James. But the fact of the matter is that Alan Kerr will not preside over the meeting. OK?"

"Well, just so long as that's clearly understood there will be no problem," James blustered, clearly unsettled and having to re-group his thoughts before trying to explain this surprise news to his fellow plotters.

"I'll be . . . er . . . I'll be going," he stammered, as he barged out of the room without further comment.

When Bill came out he almost bumped into Alan, who had just arrived. He quickly gave him a review of his conversation with James Frame. Alan patted his shoulder and said they would be praying for wisdom for him during the meeting.

The church hall was filling up quickly and a buzz of lively conversation arose from the gathering. Ron and Jack Kemp were seated near the front. Mrs. Shearer and Martha sat with Ruth Morgan in the middle of the hall. Tim and Sally Robson sat near the neutral zone that separated the two factions. In the back area James Frame and his wife Jean were surrounded on every side with supporters. These included quite a few people who were practically strangers to the regular members.

A plain table and chair were set in front of the pulpit. James Frame had been so relieved at discovering Alan would not be officiating that he had expressed no objections to Bill taking on the role.

The black hands on the plain white dial of the large clock in the hall reached the fateful time of 7:30 p.m. The church hall was nearly full. There had never been such an attendance at a prayer meeting in the living memory of any members of Earlton Baptist Church.

Bill rose from his seat on the front row and made his way to the table from which he addressed the members.

"Friends, we will take the opportunity to ask the Lord's help for our business this evening by opening our gathering in prayer."

He carried a sheaf of paper on which his fingers opened and closed nervously and revealed the anxiety he was trying desperately to hide. He almost knocked over the glass of water

172

on the table as he laid the papers down. He was alarmed to see just how much his hands trembled.

As Bill looked across the crowded rows he was amazed to see Phil Wilson sitting over to the right, near the front. He could hardly believe it, but it suddenly calmed him for some unknown reason and he had an inner certainty that Phil was there as a supporter. This observation greatly encouraged him as he rose to his feet to open the meeting in prayer. He was quite adequate in his petitions and had largely regained his composure by the time he finished praying.

Bill was unsure of how the meeting should be conducted and was trusting that many of the prayers of the saints would be remembered by the Lord at this time.

"If all their faithful petitions don't cause the Lord to give me wisdom and direction now for this meeting, I'm sunk," he thought dolefully. In another glance across the hall he saw the two old sisters looking as calm and serene as if they were sitting in the back room of the book shop with their favorite cup of tea. This also was a great blessing to him as he began to feel that he had quite a few friends in the meeting.

Clearing his throat anxiously, Bill began to address the meeting.

"You are all aware no doubt of the reasons for this special business meeting. This was requested by a sufficient number of the members to enable it to be called." Bill paused, before continuing. "Our brother, Deacon James Frame, has been nominated to speak on behalf of those who requested the meeting. I think it would be good at this point to call on him to speak and bring any motion that he, and those of like mind, wish to be considered by the membership this evening."

Bill sat down and, mopping his head with a white handkerchief, surprised at how wet with sweat the handkerchief was as he returned it to his pocket.

173

James Frame rose to speak, stepping into the aisle adjacent to where he was sitting. He had several papers in his hand to which he referred briefly before he began to speak.

"My dear friends and fellow members," he began with an ingratiating voice and in fawning manner. "My dear friends, only the Lord knows how much it has grieved me and those of like mind, good ordinary reliable church members of long standing, to have to come here this evening to raise such matters." He nodded his head slowly, pausing for dramatic effect and giving the impression that he was about to break down in tears.

Ron sat diagonally across the hall from him and he glared at James Frame with less than affection as James continued to put on his show of contrition and concern.

"Those of you who have known me over my many years of, I trust, faithful service will know that I have the interest of this church in my heart above everything else." He looked over his half spectacles for some mark of approval at this announcement, but it was noticeable that he looked directly at his own supporters in the back rows, carefully avoiding eye contact with the opposition.

Raising his voice, suddenly James thundered, "The church is facing a crisis! Discontent with the present form of administration is rampant among a majority of members."

"I have to say this," his voice dropping to almost a whisper, "and, oh, how it grieves me to do so, but it must be said." Then measuring his words carefully for maximum effect he intoned, "How can we come to any other conclusion, however reluctantly, than that there is some plot or scheme to wrest our beloved church from us by those particularly who are newcomers and to whom we voluntarily entrusted important office and responsibility in all good faith. Is this the Christian way?" He appealed in as close to a majestic utterance as

174

he was able to conjure up.

Several murmurs of approval emanated from the back rows at this, in their estimation, masterful oratory!

The Smith family, Nigel and Marjorie and their two older daughters Anna and Michelle, were sitting near the middle of the hall. Nigel was a "fence sitter" and had not displayed any allegiance to either of the protagonists. He could be swayed in any direction if the arguments were persuasive enough.

Michelle Smith, a student like her older sister Anna, was developing into a reasonably keen Christian with definite views of her own. She was active in the Christian Union at the university and had become favorably inclined toward Alan's ministry although she had not vocalized this at home or in the church. She was studying English literature for her degree and was at this particular time examining the works of several poets, including Scotland's national bard, Robert Burns.

"This is no coincidence surely?" Michelle thought. "I have been reading and studying *Holy Willie's Prayer* in my class studies this very week." As she listened intently to James Frame's peremptory statement, her mind flashed back to a couple of verses she found uncannily accurate in summing up her feelings of his oration.

> Yet I am here a chosen sample,
> To show thy grace is great and ample;
> I'm here a pillar in thy temple, strong as a rock,
> A guide, a buckler, an' example To a' thy flock.

James Frame felt he had carried the day! It was now time to propose his motion which he was confident would be approved.

"I now propose . . ." He paused, peering over the half spectacles with steely gaze. "I now propose the motion, that we remove Mr. Alan Kerr from all pastoral duties and responsibilities as of now, and set up a vacancy committee to pursue the matter of the urgent appointment of a proper pastor."

"Hear, hear," shouted his supporters as he returned to his seat with a smile of smug satisfaction across his face.

Bill nodded wanly in acknowledgment. Before he could inquire if there was a second to the motion, a voice shouted from the midst of the Frame camp. "I second the motion!" It was Roger Drury, a key supporter of James Frame.

Bill acknowledged the second to the motion and asked, "Are there any other motions?"

After a brief silence, a quiet voice rose near the front. Many of the members at the back of the hall half rose to their feet to see who was speaking.

"I want to propose we reject the previous motion and consider the installation of our Brother Alan Kerr as pastor of Earlton Baptist Church."

A gasp of astonishment rippled through the hall.

"It's Phil Wilson!" The whispered comments passed from one to another up and down every row.

"If I may, Mr. Chairman and friends, have opportunity just for a moment to elaborate on my proposal. As many of you know, my wife and I supported the motion against Mr. Kerr fairly recently. Perhaps like many gathered here tonight, I respectfully suggest, we were not fully cognizant of the issues at stake. We were swayed by the assertions of Mr. Frame without giving much thought as to any biblical basis for these. I realize that this is not the time for sermonizing, which I am certainly not adequate to engage upon. However, I feel *very* strongly about this issue and crave your patience for a moment or two. First, I pose a question. What single piece of biblical evidence did James Frame bring to underscore his allegations against the character of our Brother Kerr? Second, what definitive acts or conduct does he feel that Alan Kerr has scripturally violated? If he now proposes to bring these up, we might skeptically inquire why we were not afforded the opportunity to consider them at the time of his motion? To make such allegations without the evidence or facts to substantiate is, I respectfully suggest, tantamount to a slander on the character of our Brother Kerr. Therefore, I propose the rejection of Mr. Frame's motion."

The audience was thunderstruck, the atmosphere electric. Bill was dazed but he quickly silenced several opposing voices that sought to air their views without proper reference to the chair.

"Are there any seconds to this motion?" he asked, with an inner sense that perhaps things were not going the way James Frame and his band had thought they would.

Several members rose simultaneously to second the motion and Bill faced a dilemma in deciding which one to accept. Ron was certainly one of the first to jump up with his hand raised aloft. Bill was reluctant, however, to accept his proposal because he suspected that Ron would launch into a personal tirade against James Frame. Another figure, whose identity Bill did not instantly recognize in the gloomy lighting, stood close to Ron. Bill thought it would be best to recognize him and receive his motion.

"Yes, brother!" he said authoritatively.

"I second Phil Wilson's counter-motion."

Bill felt a little stab of apprehension as he recognized the voice. "Oh . . . er . . . yes . . eh . . . Jack Kemp seconds the counter-motion!"

Unsure of the proper protocol for conducting business meetings, Bill longed for the termination of the gathering. When Jack asked leave to explain his support for the counter-motion, Bill wearily waved him to continue but with the admonition that time now demanded that he be brief.

"I will certainly be brief," Jack began nervously. Although he was inexperienced in these matters, he quickly went to the heart of the issue and expressed his view.

"I have a question which will explain my unqualified support for this motion of opposition," he began. Looking down he saw Ron's eager face radiating agreement even before he began to explain his reasons.

"My question is, how can any person who claims to be a Christian be so obstinately opposed to a man of God trying to implement God's principles in a church which claims to be evangelical?"

A hubbub arose and James Frame stood immediately in protest to this statement, his face red with anger.

"How dare a young upstart like you—" James' voice was drowned out by the furor that ensued.

Bill frantically waved his papers, demanding order. Strangely in the midst of it all, however, he found himself thinking, "Jack's quite right!"

Several minutes elapsed before Bill could calm the tempest sufficiently to make himself heard. When the noise subsided Bill spoke firmly, "We will now take a vote on these motions. On the motion proposed by Mr. James Frame, those in favor, please raise your hands."

A number of hands quickly shot up, followed by a couple which were lifted somewhat hesitatingly. Bill asked two of the brethren to count the votes and bring the total to him. He wrote it down before saying, "On the counter-motion proposed by Mr. Phil Wilson, those in favor please raise your hands."

Again the appointed men counted the hands and brought the total to Bill with a bit of solemnity.

"I hereby announce the result of the voting," Bill said loudly.

Clearing his throat and trying not to give any clue as to the result of the vote, he announced to the silent congregation, "For the motion by Mr. James Frame, 38 votes!"

A gasp rose from the audience and it was impossible to ascertain which of the camps was responsible.

"For the counter-motion by Mr. Phil Wilson, 40 votes!" Uninhibited cheering broke out in the vicinity of Ron and Jack's row.

Several people crowded around Alan and Carol, who had remained outside the hall during the heated proceedings. They embraced them joyfully. Jack and Ron were practically dancing in the aisle while the two old sisters allowed themselves the indulgence of a beaming smile.

James Frame was livid. He stomped out the door with his cronies and hurled a final anathema over his shoulder as he defiantly asserted, "You have not heard the last of this matter."

19

Ten lepers were healed . . . only one went back to give thanks

Mrs. Shearer and Martha Wood were surrounded by Alan's numerous supporters who were overjoyed at the result of the meeting. Because of confusion, the abrupt ending of the proceedings, and the angry departure of James Frame and his brigade, the business meeting had not lasted as long as anticipated.

"Now if you can all hear me above this din," Martha shouted good-naturedly, "Mrs. Shearer and I want as many of you as are free, to come back to the book shop for tea and fellowship with us."

"Yes, yes," Mrs. Shearer said excitedly. "Alan, you and Carol and these younger ones and any others please come along. There's no excuse now that the meeting at the church ended so early."

Ron had suddenly noticed with a degree of interest that Michelle Smith had seemed pleased with the outcome of things. He had only known her casually through her attending church with her parents, but she seemed to have blossomed into a very attractive young lady since starting studies at the university. Ignoring the general melee of folks milling around and excitedly discussing the evening's events, Ron decided to go over and speak to her.

"Hi, Michelle." Ron greeted her as nonchalantly as possible, but as he drew nearer to her he was unexpectedly overcome by the beauty of this dark-haired young lady.

Quickly composing himself, he asked, "What do you think about the meeting?"

She smiled, being quite flattered at his attention. "Well, it was a real surprise, I must say. But I'm glad it worked out that way," she said with a touch of defiance in her voice.

Ron guessed that it was probably because her father had appeared non-committal about the whole affair.

"Michelle, my dear," Martha Wood's voice rang in their ears, "we're going to have a little time together with some of the friends at the book shop and we'd like you to come as well."

"Thank you, Miss Wood. I'll let my parents know where I'm going."

"You, too, Ron," Martha said, noticing that it took a moment for him to snap out of his trance-like gaze at Michelle and give a reply.

"Oh . . . er . . . yes, sure, thanks," Ron blurted out, blushing a little as he turned around to face Martha.

"Come along then," she said in her motherly way. "Jack and the others are already on their way to the book shop with Mrs. Shearer."

It was crowded in the little back room of the shop, but there was a buoyant, lighthearted atmosphere and no one minded being crowded in the small room.

Mrs. Shearer said in the midst of the crowd, "Now, friends, we're glad that you are all here and before we go any further I have a little announcement to make. This has been a memorable day in many ways. In some ways, sad. In other ways, glad. But Martha and I have our own little surprise to reveal to you. We have decided, as she practically lives here as it is, that we are going to share this small house behind the book shop and it will save her tramping back and forth every day. We have two little rooms and it seems the sensible thing to do. We're not getting any younger, you know!"

Everyone laughed and shouted their approval of this arrangement.

"Now, Alan," she continued, "will you give thanks to the Lord for these mercies before us? Then we can all have a nice cup of tea together. I'm sure we're all dying for one after the excitement of this day."

Ron and Michelle, apparently lost in their own little isolated world, were oblivious to the hubbub of animated conversation about them.

After some time, Mrs. Shearer rattled a teaspoon on her saucer, to get the attention of the group.

"I want to ask the indulgence of our pastor—" She paused before continuing. "I want to ask dear Brother Alan if I might be permitted to say something which is on my heart at this moment."

With a twinkle in her eye, she assured them that she had no intention of preaching. They all laughed and Alan waved her on.

"This is a solemn and a joyous day. We need to pray for our friends who have been unsympathetic with our desires, and we believe, the will of God. But there is a great danger of which we need to be reminded. Since the conclusion of the meeting I have been greatly impressed with the narrative of the ten lepers in Luke 17. Is it in our hearts before we proceed with anything else, before we ask for any other requests, to return to the Lord with great gratitude for His intervention on our behalf?"

The gathering quickly sobered and quietened down as she continued to speak. She was not preaching. The Bible lay in her hand as she quietly unfolded the burden of her soul.

"Ten lepers were marvelously healed. 'Jesus, Master, have mercy on us,'[71] they cried in desperation. But we find incredibly, that only one went back to give thanks. Do you not think that this is sadly typical of many churches and many Christian people?"

There was a decided hush in the room. Alan nodded seriously at Mrs. Shearer's last point.

"Are we so excited at the favorable outcome of the day, in our estimation, that we have little thought of thanking the Lord for His great condescension toward us?" The conviction grew deeper by the moment.

"Where are the nine?" she asked with some vehemence, startling the hearers.

There was rapt attention now. Bill looked at her with almost devout intensity, the tumultuous events of the day receding in the reality of the present. Even Ron was temporarily detached from Michelle's spell, as the godly old saint unburdened her heart. Jack felt a pang of conviction because this had so often been his testimony—*ingratitude!*

Mrs. Shearer, suddenly conscious of the electric atmosphere, became apologetic as she nervously exclaimed, "Oh dear, I am going on a bit, aren't I? Let me sit down. I sometimes get carried away when things press in upon me."

She started to apologize again, but Alan interrupted her. "Sister, you have no need to apologize. The reminder you have given us is from the Lord. We are the ones who should be apologizing, first to the Savior, and then to dear folks like you who display much more sensitivity to the Spirit's leading than we do. Let's pray before we break up and go home."

Alan thanked the Lord for His interventions, and prayed,

"Dear God, please help those who left the meeting in opposition. Again we thank thee for giving Phil Wilson such courage in coming and taking a stand for truth. We all know how difficult this must have been for him to do, in spite of his personal distress and anxiety over Gwen's condition."

Jack observed that Ron had left the book shop with Michelle Smith and without any parting word to him, an action hitherto unthinkable. Still he smiled and comforted himself with the thought that this would make his introduction of Alice at the church on Sunday a little easier. His uneasiness over any secretive activity he had engaged upon without Ron's knowledge, quickly dissipated.

As Alan and Carol settled into the front seats of the car to drive home after an eventful day, Alan was very quiet and pensive. Carol did not disturb his reverie and patiently waited for him to reveal what was on his mind. Eventually he said, "Carol, it's just like the Lord, I suppose, to bring good out of ignorance and bad intent."

"What are you talking about?" she asked quizzically.

"Didn't you notice?" he replied in a teasing fashion.

"No, I didn't. I mean *what* should I have noticed?"

"Well, praise the Lord, that's marvelous!"

Carol's voice rose in frustration. "Alan Kerr, will you tell me what on earth you are talking about?"

"Carol," he said in a rather relieved tone, "Carol, the meeting, the vote, that's not the way to conduct church business. We should never be carrying a matter of such major importance, or any importance for that matter, on a two vote majority."

"Well, I never!" Carol replied with some incredulity.

"That's what prayerlessness, biblical ignorance, and lack of spirituality can bring you to. I will certainly be striving earnestly, if God will help me, to change that situation."

"In what way?"

"Well, to seek to promote such a spirit of unity, harmony, and spirituality in the church that we can come to harmonious resolutions by mutual consent without the need of voting."

"I certainly look forward to that day," Carol said drowsily. "But I'm sure a lot happier now than I was when we left earlier tonight to go to the meeting."

20

'Blest be the tie that binds' has become a meaningless phrase

A new air of anticipation prevailed as the congregation of Earlton Baptist Church made their way to the worship service on Sunday morning. Truly, a few familiar faces were missing as they gathered and this occasioned sorrow in hearts now unfettered from the burdens of recent months.

Ron sat next to Michelle Smith quite openly although Jack was apparently still permitted to occupy his seat next to him on the other side.

As Jack looked around the church just before Alan went into the pulpit he thought, "It's so sad to see the empty spaces where families once sat. Still it's comforting that it is not as bad as I'd feared, and in truth the place still looks reasonably filled. I don't see Tim and Sally Robson though." A thought of concern flashed through his mind.

The service had a good sense of liberty as Alan preached with divine assistance.

* * *

Jack had arranged to meet Alice in the public park close

by the church and then to go on to the evening Gospel service. The old sisters had promised to pray, he had prayed himself, and Alan had assured him that he would also be praying, so he felt greatly encouraged.

He arrived at the public park about half an hour before he had arranged to meet Alice. He was strolling around, enjoying looking at the scenery when he saw Tim Robson. He hurried over to greet him, but sensed that Tim wasn't overjoyed to see him.

"Hi, Tim," he said cheerily. "I've missed you the last few days."

"Oh, yes," Tim stumbled a little, "I've been busy and. . . ."

He seemed to grope for the next sentence as Jack broke in, "Is everything OK?"

Before Tim could answer, Jack continued, "What did you think of that meeting, eh? I've been praising the Lord ever since. Haven't you?"

"Well, no. I'm afraid I haven't."

"What!" Jack exploded. "Why not?"

"Well, actually Sally and I won't be coming back to the church."

"You're joking," Jack said incredulously. "Why not?"

"I'd rather not say, but let's put it this way—we haven't been happy there for some time now."

"Have you told Alan?" Jack pressed.

"Well, not yet, but I will. I'd be glad if you kept this to yourself meantime."

Jack was exasperated and angry by now as he thought, "Yes, sure, but you better tell Alan pretty soon because I'm not promising to keep this hidden for very long."

He saw Alice approaching and what should have been a very enjoyable evening was now soured by this encounter with Tim Robson.

Jack was muttering under his breath about "spineless wimps" when Alice arrived.

"Hi, Jack," Alice said brightly, as Jack sought to hide his feelings.

"Hi, Alice! Great to see you." She looked really attractive and this helped to assuage the anger that smoldered in Jack after his conversation with Tim.

* * *

There was a good attendance at the Sunday night Gospel service and Jack noticed one or two new faces in the congregation. He saw Ron and Michelle sitting over to the right. Ron had not yet seen Jack.

Just then he did, and Jack nearly laughed out loud at the look on Ron's face when he saw Alice sitting beside him. Ron gave a cheery nod and immediately leaned over to talk to Michelle. Jack guessed that it had nothing to do with the impending Gospel service.

Mrs. Shearer and Martha Wood, seeming more aglow than ever, sat next to Phil Wilson. Jack momentarily wondered how Phil was managing to attend with Gwen being so ill.

These thoughts were quickly dispelled as Alan rose and announced the first hymn.

* * *

It had been a powerful message. Alan preached from the text, "How shall we escape, if we neglect so great salvation?"[72] Jack could sense that Alice had been greatly affected and might even be shedding tears, but he dared not look to confirm this.

189

He prayed inwardly that it might be so. Although he was attracted to Alice, Jack knew the principle reason for bringing her to church was that she might be confronted with the Gospel. Any relationship afterward would be in God's hand to direct.

Alan concluded by saying, "If anyone wants to discuss or ask anything concerning the message, I will be available at the end of the service."

Jack glanced sideways and sure enough, Alice *was* weeping softly.

"Would you like to speak to Alan about anything?" Jack whispered quietly.

Alice nodded. They walked to the back of the church where Alan was shaking hands with members who were now leaving. Jack introduced Alice to Alan, who invited them to come into the vestry.

None of this had escaped the attention of the two mothers in Israel, who bowed their heads in silent prayer. Noticing this, Bill and Ruth did likewise.

When Alice came out of the vestry, nobody needed to be told what had happened. Like Moses of old, her face revealed the story.[73] Jack hugged her in front of the others gathered there. Then realizing what he had done he hastily withdrew his embrace and sought to regain his composure in as dignified a manner as possible. Alice was so overjoyed that she hardly noticed his enthusiasm.

The old sisters, Bill and Ruth, Ron and Michelle, Alan and Carol, and one or two others who had waited behind shook Alice's hand and embraced her.

Jack was in orbit! But suddenly his joy faded. He recalled the afternoon's conversation with Tim Robson. Thinking that time might be of the essence, he drew Alan aside and quickly informed him of Tim's intentions.

He began seriously, "I hope you don't feel that I'm speaking behind Tim's back, but it's been worrying me ever since."

Alan's countenance fell as Jack related the afternoon's events.

"That's bad news, Jack. Thanks for bringing it to my attention. You can rest assured that your genuine concern for the Robsons' spiritual welfare overrules any supposed breaking of confidence."

Alan felt a bit of good news would lighten the scene so he suddenly cried out, "Mrs. Shearer, dear sister, share with the friends here that wonderful piece of news you gave me immediately after the close of the service." He explained that he would have shared it with the whole church, but the two sisters were delayed somewhat in coming to the evening service.

The whole group focused their undivided attention on Mrs. Shearer and waited for an explanation of what was exciting Alan. They already were overjoyed at Alice's conversion. What else could it be?

"Now, just listen!" he said frustratingly. "Mrs. Shearer will explain everything in an instant."

"My dears," Mrs. Shearer beamed, "we were visiting Gwen Wilson this afternoon when her doctor came to the house. He explained that he normally would never call on a Sunday, but that he had just received a report the previous day. Because of extreme pressure at work he had not been able to contact the Wilsons sooner, but he wanted to speak to them in person so he went to their home. The cancer is definitely in remission and though the doctor could not make any forecast or promises, he felt that it was a massive improvement over her recent expectations."

After a few moments of an unrestrained outburst of cheering and hugging at this marvelous news, Alan said, "Perhaps our Brother Bill would return thanks to the Lord briefly for the wonderful blessings we have experienced this day and then we can all make our way home."

* * *

It was around eleven in the morning when Alan heard the front door bell ring. He didn't usually go to the church on Mondays so he was occasionally visited informally by members of the congregation and he concluded this is what would be in store.

Tim Robson, looking somewhat sheepish and apprehensive but also manifesting an attitude of defiance, was standing on the doorstep when Alan opened the door. Alan invited him to come in.

When they sat down, Tim, a rather sparse figure with glasses and a wispy beard, cleared his throat and said, "I've come to inform you that Sally and I won't be coming back to the church anymore."

"Why in the world not?" Alan asked.

"Well," Tim began, fidgeting as he spoke and avoiding Alan's gaze, "we've not been happy in the church for some time so we feel it would be better to find another church to attend."

"May I ask the source of your unhappiness?" Alan asked directly.

"Well, er . . . it's not . . . I mean . . . It's a few things," Tim finally got out.

"Such as?" Alan pressed.

"Well . . ." he began again, as if the word *well* was a kind of pause which enabled him to gather his thoughts for the next momentous statement. "Well, it's you, Alan. I don't think you have been handling things in a loving manner and

192

this has offended some people."

"That's a distinct possibility, Tim. I'm very conscious actually of my shortcomings in this area. However, I'm encouraged to think that you have no doubt been praying that God would help me to have more wisdom and grace in these matters."

Tim quickly shifted his eyes at this and continued without reference to Alan's statement.

"Anyway, Sally and I would be happier in another church and I just wanted to let you know we won't be back."

"Would you mind me asking you, Tim, if you could just give me the specific biblical principles that undergird your taking this very serious step of leaving a local church? It would also be of interest to me to know roughly how many biblical grounds the New Testament sets out as a basis for leaving one's local church?"

Tim studiously avoided response to Alan's questions, but added that he thought Alan's conduct as a pastor was too dictatorial.

Alan then asked him which particular church he felt called to attend. Tim replied that they would be "looking around" first before they made up their minds. When Alan pressed him whether he thought this was a biblical way of resolving such an important matter, Tim stirred and half rose to leave as Alan pinned him with a final barb.

"Tim!" he said strongly. "You are taking the serious step of leaving your local church in violation of biblical principles. You are trivializing the whole concept of biblical church membership. What manner of fellowship is it that can be so easily broken by irritations, trifles, and minor disagreements?"

Tim was on his feet now, flustered, convicted, and desperately wanting to get out of this embarrassing predicament.

"Have I been preaching heresy?" Alan asked further.

"No, no, it's . . . er . . . It's not that. Look, Alan I have to go now. Thanks for listening. I'll see you around."

"No, sorry, Tim. I don't think you will. We haven't seen you or Sally at the prayer meetings recently. You haven't been inclined to hear my plea that you remain in the fellowship of God's people here in your local church. You've not explained how you will react if the pastor of the next church you join displays characteristics of which you disapprove. You have rejected authority, both of the Scriptures and of the church, and in doing so you have manifested divisive propensities.[74] Sadly, you leave us no alternative but to consider your previous protestations of desire for Christian fellowship and identification with us here to be nothing more or less than shallow pretense. 'Blest be the tie that binds,' has become a meaningless phrase, and 'We bear our mutual burdens,' just tinkling cymbals and sounding brass.[75]

"Tim, please consider these principles. I know you want to go now, but I'm pleading with you, not only for your own sake, but for Sally and the baby's sake, and for the unity of the church. Don't defect from the cause of God here at Earlton Baptist Church."

"Well, thanks, Alan, but I really must go. Sorry I can't change my mind. All the best. Good-bye!"

Alan felt so discouraged, especially after the blessings of the day before. He sat in his chair and pondered.

"Sadly, we seldom find those with an attitude like Tim, who, are ever restrained from their error by biblical pleading. It appears that they have already overthrown biblical principle in the very act of coming to such superficial conclusions."

"Is it the case," Alan thought, "that Christians generally have little notion of spiritual love beyond that friendly feeling which exists among the members of an earthly society?"[76]

He was beginning to realize the magnitude of the task he faced in leading the members of Earlton Baptist Church to a place of mutual love, responsibility, and accountability, and to a true place of unity of the saints and brotherly affection. Where this can be easily broken, he thought, it is doubtful if it ever truly existed.

21

Lord, teach us to pray

Bill and Ruth were reminiscing as they made their way to the prayer meeting.

"A lot has surely happened around here since I was summoned to that meeting at Andrew's house and he announced his intended removal," Bill said, shaking his head.

"Can you believe what's happened in that short space of time?" Ruth asked. "It's beyond belief. If someone were writing a book about it you would think it was an exaggeration."

"No doubt about that, Ruth, but I'm praising the Lord for all of it nevertheless."

"Look, Bill!" Ruth said excitedly as they drove into the church parking lot.

"Take it easy, Ruth. You just about startled me out of my wits. What are you talking about anyway?"

"Look! Look!" she said even more emphatically as she pointed to the other side of the parking lot.

"Well, blow me down!" Bill exclaimed in disbelief.

There walking a little unsteadily, but walking and smiling, was Gwen Wilson on the arm of her husband Phil.

"Gwen!" Ruth cried out as tears trickled down her cheek, "what are you doing here? You shouldn't be out yet."

"What!" Gwen retorted. "After all that's been happening in this church and in our lives. There's no way I'd have stayed at home tonight. Anyway, I'm feeling really good."

The two ladies hugged and chatted noisily as they entered the church. Everyone crowded around Gwen and made a fuss as Alan quietly told Phil how much he appreciated his courage in coming out to the business meeting the previous week.

Alan's voice boomed above the excited hubbub that vibrated through the church hall.

"Come on, you lot," he chided good-naturedly, "I've made an exception this once about starting on time, but if we don't get some order here we'll not have a meeting tonight."

They made their way to the various seats and Alan was pleasantly surprised at the good attendance, in spite of the absence of the defectors. He looked around the hall quickly.

"Well, well," he thought. "Now there's a surprise, Nigel and Marjorie Smith. Great! And who would have imagined that Michelle would be here sitting next to Ron?" Alan was unable to restrain a smile of delight.

"There are Jack and Alice. Wonderful! Good old Bill and Ruth, ever faithful." A tear started in Alan's eye as he gazed at Mrs. Shearer and Martha Wood. "Ah, Lord, what have I done to deserve such choice souls as these to fellowship with?"

He was about to give out the first hymn when he almost exclaimed audibly, "I don't believe it! Albert Higgins! He must have come to the wrong place. Good old Albert, bless his soul, he's sitting there as though nothing had ever happened in the past weeks."

At that moment Alan asked the congregation to turn to Psalm 9:10. He began to read, "And they that know thy name will put their trust in thee: for thou, LORD, hast not forsaken

198

them that seek thee."

Ron uttered a fairly unrestrained, "Amen!"

Alan smiled to himself as he went on, "I have been reading an old book and I thought this excerpt would encourage your hearts as it did mine."

He then read:

> If thou knowest and wilt believe this, this kind of knowledge and persuasion cannot but breed confidence and resolution, and consequently quiet in the heart. We dare trust a friend whose faithfulness we have tried, and we rest upon that which we know by the sure card of experience. The promises of God are all of them as true as the Gospel. Seek from one end of the heaven to the other, turn all the Bible over; and see if ever any man leaned on the promise, and the Lord did not perform what he had promised for good of his soul.[77]
>
> To bring this element of pleading the promises of God into our intercessions is something we have to try and learn. What use is it, if we have received a measure of faith but it has become emaciated through lack of use? Sin ever seeks to quench and oppose faith and negate obedience. So even as we come to engage in prayer, there is much we need to strive against. The flesh and our enemy, the devil, hate prayer. We have the command of God: "Men ought always to pray and not to faint."[78] Many and varied are the efforts of men to please God, but neither this prayer meeting, any service of the church, nor good works rendered by its members can in any wise substitute for the exercise of faith. Listen carefully to this verse in Hebrews chapter 11:6: "But without faith it is impossible to please Him."

Alan paused to underline the word *impossible* with singular emphasis.

"Impossible!" he rapped out with definite force. "Impossible! Notice that it does not say that it's possible to please Him a little by any great efforts, orthodoxy or even with fervent prayers! No! It's impossible without faith. It certainly looks as if Enoch demonstrated this quality of faith for Scripture says, 'he had this testimony, that he pleased God.'[79] We must surely covet this as individuals and as a church also."

"Fervency, accuracy, brevity, faith, importunity, expectancy, reverence, humility, gratitude, pleading of the promises, holy arguments—these and much more we have considered over the past months. Lord teach us to pray, we cry again."

Alan was not deluded. For all his exhortations, spelling out the principles, reiterating the necessity of active participation, yet such was the torpor and often sluggish nature of the languid soul that he would encounter many disappointments in the quest to bring a degree of New Testament-quality intercession into the church prayer meeting.

He mused, "Have I got what it takes to persevere on a long term basis for such a goal? How few apparently are the saints who can sustain the will or effort, even by God's grace, to break through into a place of victory in the warfare of prayer.[80] How can they be convinced for example, that any facility in effectual praying can only be achieved by regular diligent practice of the sacred art?

"If the devil and the flesh are so opposed to this exercise," Alan continued to think, "then it truly must be of value beyond our understanding."

He offered an involuntary inward prayer for wisdom in the execution of his duties, with special reference to the realm of prayer.

* * *

Settled comfortably at home after the prayer meeting, Alan began thinking back over the fleeting months since they had arrived at Earlton Baptist Church. He sought to collate his thoughts in an orderly fashion as he said to Carol, "You know, there is so much work to be done, particularly in the area of prayer, and many difficulties to overcome which require a precise balance. On the one hand there is the need to stir people from sloth and complacency; on the other, the requirement not to be over fastidious in addressing minor aberrations or deviations."

Carol encouraged him by saying, "The fact is, you have spent considerable time and effort in seeking to get people just to pray. You faced the danger that having once gotten a response in this exercise, you might intimidate them to silence again by over zealousness in correction. I realize probably better than most that these matters have been a matter of genuine concern to you."

"Well, that's true, dear," Alan said thoughtfully, "but there are so many bad habits that have never been addressed and they are now going to be difficult to rectify. The way so many use the titles of God as a form of punctuation is objectionable, but a hard habit to break."

Carol interjected, "You know that book you gave me? Well I think the old writer hit the nail on the head regarding this matter. Let me find the place where he describes that type of activity. Here it is. 'They seem to furnish a kind resting place for the mind, to afford an opportunity for reflecting on what is to follow.'"[81]

Alan retorted, "I'm certainly grateful to that same writer for pertinent observations. However, there was little mentioned that I haven't observed as needing correction while we've been here at Earlton. In fact I could easily add many other failings to the list without straining my memory."

22

A praying pulpit begets praying pews

As Alan drove to the church on a bright Monday morning, he wondered what kind of response there would be to his attempt to start a ministers' fraternal for pastors of like mind as himself. Not that there were many in the vicinity who were of the same persuasion.

He arrived at the church in good time for the proposed commencement at 10:30 a.m. If two or three at best turned up this would be an encouragement as he had found it difficult to find many evangelical ministers in the town, far less those who held to the doctrines of grace. Sitting down at his desk in the study, he examined the list of five possible attendees which comprised five names.

Soon Alan heard the sound of footsteps coming towards the front door. He rose to go and greet the visitor.

"Jim Gates, pastor of Grange Road Free Church," the first person announced as he extended his hand with a warm smile. Jim was in his mid-thirties and of burly build with a ruddy complexion, fair hair, and kindly brown eyes. Alan had never met him before but had heard good reports of the stand he was taking for truth in a congregation of mixed persuasions.

"Oh, and this is a friend of mine, Pastor Alistair White," Jim continued. "Alistair is the new pastor of the Reformed Presbyterian Church on Poplar Road."

"Hi, Alistair. Good to meet you," Alan responded, shaking his hand and inviting the two men into the study. "I think there will be enough room in here for all of us," he smiled.

"How many are you expecting?" Alistair asked as he sat down facing Alan.

"Well, if we had three or four I would be quite happy," Alan replied. "There are not many who share the same convictions as we do."

Just then Alan heard someone else trying the front door so he went to greet the next arrival.

"Ah, hello, Mark," he said as he recognized Mark Shaw, the pastor of the local Baptist church on the other side of town. Alan had met Mark on several occasions and had sought to encourage him as he wrestled with many difficulties in his first charge. This was a very loose, supposedly evangelical Baptist church.

"Hi, Alan. Hope I'm not late, but you know the phone always rings just when you're ready to leave!"

"No, no. We're actually just gathering, although you may be the last one now."

Just as he was about to close the door, Alan noticed another figure approaching. He invited Mark to join the other pastors while he waited for this person to arrive. As the man came nearer Alan could see that he was a tall, rather distinguished looking gentleman, probably in his early sixties.

"I hope it's all right for me to come," the stranger said pleasantly. "My name is Derek Carson."

"Professor Derek Carson?" Alan asked with some incredulity.

"Afraid so," he replied with a smile lighting up his

crinkled countenance. "But, don't worry, I retired from the seminary several months ago and I'm just an ordinary church member now. In reality that is part of my reason for coming this morning."

Alan looked bewilderedly at him, "I, eh, I, don't quite understand."

"My wife and I have just moved into the district and we're looking for a church to attend and I've heard that you seem to preach and believe the things that we find precious. So I thought I would come and introduce myself. Maybe I can encourage you friends here by coming along."

"You certainly could Professor Carson, I—"

The professor interrupted Alan with a twinkle in his eyes, "Please. If you don't mind, just call me Derek. And your name is? . . ."

"I'm Alan Kerr! Please come in and meet the others and we'll talk about Earlton after the meeting."

Alan apologized to the others as he explained that he and Professor Carson had got caught up in conversation at the door but he now wanted to introduce them all to each other. The pastors agreed to fellowship on a first name.

"I hope that you brethren will forgive my presumptuous attitude in preparing to say something at this first meeting, but I wasn't sure who would be coming, if anyone indeed." They laughed and Alan continued, "I want the gatherings to be informal but profitable, and I will be looking to you brethren to make contributions in the days ahead, ministering to us, as God would lead."

They all nodded agreement, and Alan requested that Derek open the meeting in prayer.

"We have been going through traumatic experiences at Earlton Baptist Church as several of you have probably heard," Alan began. "However, I thought it might be good for this first gathering if I shared a few of the things that God has greatly impressed upon some of us over the past months. Perhaps something of profit will encourage you men. Prayer has been the issue that has occupied our attention, and to be honest, has caused some of the disturbance at the church."

Alan gave a resume of the main points which he had been addressing, including the shopping list, and the necessity of fervency, accuracy, brevity, and faith.

"But, men, what has come home to me as a pastor is the distinct impression that we, as the properly constituted authority in the church, have a lot to answer for in the death of the prayer meeting generally in these days."

"I was greatly struck," Alan continued to an increasingly interested audience, "by the force of that one statement in Luke 11:1. 'Lord, teach us to pray.' I realized that I had never ever been instructed how to pray in anything resembling a regular or systematic manner. It also occurred to me that in my particular knowledge, I didn't know of any fellow pastors who majored on this vital necessity. It just seemed to be that it was largely taken for granted that a person is saved and then learns to pray by attending church. When I consider that in the past months I have sought to maximize the instruction in this area to a regular weekly input which has only scratched the surface of the subject. It is only now, after considerable diligent regular exhortation that I am beginning to see the first glimmer of success and slight improvement in our corporate and individual exercise. It is a daunting task and does not surprise me that many pastors just leave it alone, though I find this inexcusable. In the estimation of many, personal praying is sacrosanct, untouchable almost beyond criticism, and therefore cannot be addressed, particularly as regards correction. I find this tragic, and probably a condition much approved by Satan. While there is some truth in the personal and private nature of prayer, this should never inhibit instruction or correction."

"Excuse me for interrupting, Alan," Mark said with deference. "This is a mighty shake up for me personally, and I'm a novice in this field I have to admit, but I want to learn all I can about this subject. So, may I ask, are the things you are suggesting not just for those who have a special gift in prayer?"

"Mark, I don't think there is any doubt that some men have been particularly gifted in prayer and far surpass us lesser mortals in this sacred exercise. However, the recognition of this does not excuse any of us from improving in that which we have certainly been commanded to engage in. 'Men ought always to pray and not to faint.'[82] Is it not also true that we recognize first the necessity, 'Physician heal thyself.'[83] 'A prayerless ministry is the undertaker for all God's truth, and for all God's church.'[84] There can be no doubt that the precept, 'Example is the best teacher' is one to be cultivated."

"Excellent admonition," Derek intervened. "If I may be allowed to say so, twenty-five years teaching in the seminary convinced me that, though we certainly need an educated ministry, yet so many of our students left college ill-equipped in the realm of experimental religion. Greek, Hebrew, hermeneutics, homiletics, important though they undoubtedly are, yet what is all of this without some ability in intercession?"

"You're absolutely right, Derek." Alan responded. "And is it not the case that we ministers are often the worst practical examples in public praying?"

"I know exactly what you mean," Jim Gates interjected. "I was at a conference last week where one brother was asked to open in prayer and he went on for about twenty minutes. It killed the meeting before it got started. But we were all supposed to pretend that it was a most spiritual exercise of great edifying quality. I feel that sometimes ministers take the attitude that, we never got asked to preach, so we'll make up for it by occupying the pulpit in lengthy, boring praying."

Jim grimaced. "Sorry, I guess I've just shattered a sacrosanct ritual! But seriously, I wouldn't mind if these men were praying by the Holy Spirit. Then they could go on all night as far as I'm concerned, but praying in their *own* spirit— brevity is the watchword!"

"You're right," Alan said with a mischievous smile. "Seems we have to submit to the phenomenon that apparently the Holy Spirit *never* leads many to pray briefly in public!"

"Thing is," Derek added, "we become so predictable that the people know when we start to pray that it is going to be lengthy and often interminable. Also they sense that these prayers are considered sacrosanct by us, therefore beyond criticism. Indeed people are often brought into a form of bondage, arising from a guilt complex produced by a censorious attitude which they have engendered to such prayer. They should often be commended that they have so cheerfully been able to endure such lengthy vain repetition without visible complaint."

"You wanted to say something, Mark?" Alan asked.

"Well, yes, I just kind of wondered if this sort of conduct doesn't turn the pulpit into a type of 'Coward's Castle' where we can find ourselves taking advantage of a captive audience?"

"That's always something I think we ought to have in mind as a possibility," Alan responded.

Alistair White had been silent during the exchanges and had sat in rapt attention as the dialogue unfolded. Finally, when the conversation lapsed for a moment, he said, "Well, I've never been involved in any discussion like this before. I don't know whether I agree with everything that's been said, or with part of what's been said. I just need time to take it in and ponder the issues which have been raised. May I say, however, that my gut reaction is that I can't come up with too many objections right now. I'm going to need time to think this through, but I have a sneaking suspicion that some radical changes are going to have to be made in my approach to prayer, both in my personal and church life. I'm a little concerned that maybe all of this could induce us to examine the prayers ascending around us in a critical, analytical fashion, instead of identifying with them, and encouraging the weak petitioners."

"Excellent point, brother," Alan said. "I fully endorse it, and would underline that we must have tolerance, understanding, and sometimes even longsuffering." He quickly went on, "We must ever seek to encourage and help, as well as correct, and certainly only take a person aside as a last resort. Let us endeavor to counsel from the pulpit and answer the vast majority of questions that arise in the believer's life through the preached word. This will save us a lot of time in counseling sessions. I believe we ought to diligently labor to make these sessions the exception, rather than the rule."

"Just look at the time!" Alan was surprised how quickly the time had flown and how much everyone seemed to have enjoyed the session.

"Before we close," he said, "may I read a brief excerpt from a book which has been a searching, deep challenge to my own soul and several of the members of my congregation."

Alan then began to read, "A praying pulpit will beget praying pews. We do greatly need someone who can set the saints to this business of praying. We are not a generation of praying saints. Non-praying saints are a beggarly gang of saints who have neither the ardor nor the beauty nor the power of saints. Who will restore this breach? The greatest will he be of reformers or apostles who can set the church to praying.'"[85]

23

Call upon me in the day of trouble: I will deliver thee

The church was crowded and a subdued buzz of excitement filled the air. Bill whispered to Ruth in hushed tones, "Never thought I'd live to see such a day. I can't believe it!"

"I should think that you won't be alone in expressing that sentiment, dear," she said quietly.

"Just look at the place, it's marvelous," Bill exclaimed. "I don't know who arranged these flowers and decorated the place. It's so tasteful, and it just seems as if it has all been done for the glory of God first and then for the wedding."

"You know, Bill," Ruth said confidentially, "I never would have believed that Jack and Alice would have taken this step before Ron and Michelle. Would you?"

"They were going with each other before Ron and Michelle got together, but you're probably right. I would have thought Ron would have been first down the aisle, but he is Jack's best man."

"I know," Ruth said with rising excitement in her voice, "and can you imagine Ron and Michelle announcing *their* engagement this week, too? I can hardly believe it!"

"As good a time as any I suppose," he said nonchalantly.

"Bill Morgan!" Ruth expostulated in mock indignation. "Have you no romance left in your soul?"

He smiled and patted her arm.

"Hey, look at our venerable prayer warriors," Bill said, nodding toward the front of the church where the two old ladies sat in all their finery, which obviously had been stored away carefully for such auspicious occasions.

"Martha, can you believe the goodness of the Lord?" Mrs. Shearer said quietly.

Martha looked at her with a face wreathed in smiles. "I'm so excited I can hardly contain myself. I just feel like shouting out, 'Glory! Hallelujah!'"

"But you wouldn't, would you, dear?" Mrs. Shearer said a trifle anxiously as she looked around the crowded church.

"No, of course not," Martha smiled, adding a quick rejoinder, "but I certainly feel like it! I don't know whether I was more excited when Brother Alan was inducted into the pastorate, or right now as these lovely young people who are rooted and grounded in the Lord Jesus Christ come together in holy matrimony."

Mrs. Shearer brushed away a tear that was slowly trickling down her crinkled face and said, "Peter would have rejoiced to see such a day." Continuing one of the very few references to her late husband, she remarked, "But the Lord had even better plans for Peter than this day, wonderful though it is."

Martha gently took her hand and squeezed it softly but said nothing.

* * *

"That was a wonderful day, Alan," Carol said when they eventually got back home after the wedding reception. "I can't believe it. Everything went off so well, and I really believe that the Lord was glorified in everything. It was just marvelous! Those two old choice saints came close to stealing the bride's thunder though! Weren't they magnificent? Only God knows how much their prayers brought about such an occasion."

"No doubt about it," Alan said thoughtfully. "It was the turning point in the battle when God in His condescension sent them into the midst. On the human plane, we owe so much to their influence and example. Where can we begin to praise the Lord for His mercies when we saw Gwen Wilson sitting there with an inner radiance that I know must have sprung out of gratitude to God. That verse in Psalm 50 has been running through my mind for days now: 'Offer unto God thanksgiving; and pay thy vows unto the most High: And call upon me in the day of trouble: I will deliver thee, and thou shalt glorify me.' That just about sums it all up for me," Alan said reverently.

* * *

"Another Wednesday," Alan was saying to Carol as they prepared to go to the prayer meeting. "Oh, there goes the phone. Will you answer it, Carol, while I get my Bible and the car keys?"

"Yes, he's right here," Carol said, a little edge in her voice. "Alan, it's for you."

"What!" Alan exclaimed in a shocked voice. "Right. I'll be down immediately."

"What's wrong, Alan?" Carol asked, sensing something ominous.

213

"I've got to get to the church right now. That was the police. The church is on fire! It's raging out of control and they don't give much hope of saving anything."

Footnotes

[1] *The Essentials of Prayer.* E. M. Bounds. Baker Book House.
[2] James 5:16
[3] 1 Thessalonians 1:5
[4] Hebrews 4:2
[5] *The Essentials of Prayer.* E. M. Bounds. Baker Book House.
[6] *Commentary on Matthew.* William Hendricksen. p. 702. Banner of Truth.
[7] Revelation 3:20
[8] Ephesians 6:18
[9] Matthew 18:19
[10] James 4:2
[11] Luke 6:38; 2 Corinthians 9:6
[12] Romans 9:13; Romans 9:16
[13] *Body of Divinity.* p. 55. John Gill. Primitive Baptist Seminary.
[14] *Sovereignty of God.* A. W. Pink. Banner of Truth.
[15] Philippians 4:6,7
[16] Matthew 18:18,19
[17] 1 Samuel 1:15
[18] Isaiah 65:24
[19] Matthew 6:7
[20] Luke 11:1
[21] Philippians 4:6.
[22] *The Necessity of Prayer.* E. M. Bounds. Baker Book House.
[23] *Power Through Prayer.* E. M. Bounds. Marshall Morgan & Scott.
[24] *The Necessity of Prayer.* p. 55.
[25] Zechariah 12:10.
[26] *The Essentials of Prayer.* E. M. Bounds. p. 9. Baker Book House.
[27] James 4:3
[28] Matthew 6:7
[29] Banner of Truth. p. 19.
[30] Romans 8:26
[31] Isaiah 59:2
[32] Psalm 95:6
[33] Job 14:1
[34] 1 Peter 3:14
[35] Genesis 27:22
[36] Acts 15:18
[37] James 4:3
[38] 1 Kings 18:26
[39] Romans 14:22
[40] Larger Catechism.
[41] Romans 11:36
[42] 1 Corinthians 10:31
[43] Luke 11:8,9
[44] Ephesians 6:18
[45] James 1:6,7
[46] James 5:16

47 James 3:32
48 John 16:33
49 *Counsels and Thoughts.* Thos. Moor, Jas. Nisbet & Co. p. 280
50 Luke 8:23,24
51 *Christian Hymns.* Evangelical Movement of Wales. Hymn 801.
52 *The Necessity of Prayer.* E. M. Bounds. Baker Book House.
53 James 5:16
54 Luke 11:5
55 Matthew 6:7
56 Hebrews 12:6
57 John 11:3
58 Romans 8:28
59 *Counterfeit Miracles.* B. B. Warfield. Banner of Truth. p. 175.
60 Isaiah 66:2
61 *The Reign of Grace.* Abraham Booth. p. 48. Bible Truth Depot
62 *The Still Hour.* Austin Phelps. p. 20. Banner of Truth.
63 A. W. Pink. Baker Book House.
64 James 4:2
65 Ephesians 6:18
66 *The Power of Prayer.* R. A. Torrey. p. 12. Zondervan Publishing House.
67 Psalm 32:8
68 Proverbs 3:6
69 *Biblical Hermeutics.* Milton Terry. p. 153. Academie Books.
70 *The Sovereignty of God.* A. W. Pink. p. 82-83. Banner of Truth Trust.
71 Luke 17:13
72 Hebrews 2:3
73 Exodus 34:29
74 Romans 16:17
75 *Tracing the True Worship of God.* W. J. Berry. p. 44. Primitive Publications.
76 *Tracing the True Worship of God.* W. J. Berry. p. 174. Primitive Publications.
77 *The Poor Doubting Christian.* Thos. Hooker. p. 105. Odom Publications.
78 Luke 18:1
79 Hebrews 11:5
80 Galatians 6:9
81 *Thoughts on Public Prayer.* Samuel Miller. p. 177. Sprinkle Publications.
82 Luke 18:1
83 Luke 4:23
84 *Power Through Prayer.* E. M. Bounds. p. 105. Marshall, Morgan and Scott.
85 *Power Through Prayer.* E. M. Bounds. p. 126. Marshall, Morgan and Scott.